Dr Arne Rubinstein (MBBS, FRACGP) has been working with teenagers and their families for over thirty years as a doctor, counsellor, mentor and facilitator of workshops. He is an expert on adolescent development and Rites of Passage. The camps and seminars he has helped create have been a key contributor to improving the wellbeing of young men and women as well as having a positive impact on their families and communities. Dr Rubinstein was the founding CEO of The Pathways Foundation, an organisation set up to run contemporary Rites of Passage for teenage boys and girls around Australia. More recently, Dr Rubinstein co-founded Uplifting Australia, a social enterprise designed to support young Australians to reach their full potential through the delivery of educational programs and improving family relationships. Dr Rubinstein has two grown sons, Jarrah and Jaden. He lives on 140 acres of spectacular bushland in northern NSW where he has created a purpose-built campsite and leadership training facility. He is a keen surfer and works part-time in emergency medicine. *The Making of Men* is his first book.

www.doctorarne.com

THE **MAKING**
OF **MEN**

DR ARNE
RUBINSTEIN

FOREWORD BY **STEVE BIDDULPH**

First published in 2013

Reprinted in 2013

Copyright © Arne Rubinstein 2013

ISBN 9781922057310 (print)

ISBN 9781922057327 (digital)

Design and typeset copyright © Xou Creative, www.xou.com.au

Cataloguing-in-publication data is available from the National Library of Australia

Printed in Australia by Griffin Press

To my sons Jarrah and Jaden, in the
time it has taken me to write this book,
I have loved sharing the journey as you
have changed from beautiful boys
into fabulous young men.

Contents

FOREWORD by Steve Biddulph.. xiii
PROLOGUE xvii

PART 1
WHAT'S HAPPENING TO OUR BOYS? xxiii

CHAPTER 1
Which way will your boy go? 1
'Lift-off' 3
What happens after lift-off? 4
Happiness and success 5
My journey 8
The big change that all boys go through 10
Modern families 11
What about girls? 13
How to use this book 13
Key Points from Chapter 1 14

CHAPTER 2
The biggest transition of all: from boy to man 15
The differences between a boy and a man 16
A boy trapped in a man's body 17
Boy or man? 18
Men **know** when they are acting like boys
(they really do)... 30

A world running on boy psychology looks like 31

Boy psychology in society 33

How we can help our sons move from boy
psychology to healthy man psychology.. 35

Key Points from Chapter 2.. 37

CHAPTER 3

Why boys muck up.. 38

The physical, emotional and spiritual roller coaster 41

Mental pressure.. 46

The role of a parent or carer 47

A young man's needs... 50

The missing link 51

Key Points from Chapter 3... 53

CHAPTER 4

Gen Zs and the digital age 54

Sex and the internet.. 57

Reality distortion and the internet 59

The digital divide 60

Dealing with technology 61

Key Points from Chapter 4... 63

PART 2

GETTING OUR BOYS READY FOR THE WORLD 65

CHAPTER 5

You can't start raising a teenager once he
actually becomes a teenager 67

How to parent young boys... 73

The whole situation is going to change 80

Key Points from Chapter 5... 81

CHAPTER 6

How to give our sons what they need 82

What sort of a teenager will your son be? 84

A healthy Personal Identity is the key 86

The Personal Identity (PI) scale 88

How to combat the influence of technology,
drugs, alcohol and peer group pressure 96

Experimentation is normal 101

Combatting depression by bringing out
the best in our young men 103

Peer pressure and the tyranny of marketing 106

Key Points from Chapter 6 109

CHAPTER 7

The critical father/son relationship 110

Fathering young men is different from fathering boys 113

My, how things change! 114

What fathers need to do 115

Bring him into your world and the world of men 116

Honour and recognise his gifts and talents 119

Create a shift in the balance of power 125

Shaming your son is the worst thing you can do 127

Single fathers 131

Gifts of a mentor 133

A warning about mentoring 137

Key Points from Chapter 7 139

CHAPTER 8

The special mother/son relationship 140

A beautiful bond 141

Mothering boys is different from mothering young men 143

If the relationship **doesn't** evolve 146

The impact on a young man's future
relationships with women 150

What does the new relationship
look like?.. 154

Respect between a mother and her son 154

Healthy, open communication 155

Single mothers 157

Key Points from Chapter 8.. 162

CHAPTER 9

The key life skills your son needs 163

Understanding privileges are connected to responsibility.......... 165

Resilience if things don't go his way.. 169

High EQ, SQ and GQ.. 171

The ability to find creative solutions to problems 174

Understanding the power of collaboration.................................. 175

Key Points from Chapter 9.. 177

CHAPTER 10

Physical health 178

Good healthy food... 178

Adequate sleep.. 180

Regular exercise 181

Time in nature 181

Key Points from Chapter 10.. 184

PART 3

RITES OF PASSAGE IN THE 21ST CENTURY 187

CHAPTER 11

A Rite of Passage story... 189

CHAPTER 12

Rites of Passage in the 21st century 201

What exactly is a Rite of Passage? 204

An event to mark a change in a person's life 205

A ritual (a custom or ceremony) 207

The Boy-to-Man Rite of Passage 208

Why we need a modern Boy-to-Man Rite of Passage 208

Rites of Passage today 210

The impact of a 21st-century Boy-to-Man Rite of Passage 216

The shift from boy psychology to healthy man psychology 221

Good mentors 222

What about boys without fathers? 222

Key Points from Chapter 12 225

CHAPTER 13

How to get involved in a 21st-century Boy-to-Man
Rite of Passage 226

Get the timing right 228

Research, plan and understand the
process as best you can 230

Enlist the help of others 230

Make sure **all** the elements are covered properly 231

Be respectful and safe 232

Key Points from Chapter 13 233

CHAPTER 14

Creating your own Boy-to-Man Rite of Passage 234

The separation 234

If time is an issue 236

The transition 237

The return 243

The role of mentors post-Rite of Passage 244

Following-up after a Rite of Passage 245

Key Points from Chapter 14 246

CONCLUSION 247

ACKNOWLEDGEMENTS... 250

PARENTING SUPPORT SERVICES

Links 256

Further reading 260

Index 262

FOREWORD by Steve Biddulph

When I was a teenager, I was shy, socially awkward and often lost in the big world I was supposed to be moving into. I was lucky to have support and care, though sometimes it was a near thing. I knew how fraught was the passage from boy to man.

All around me, other boys were having their own struggles. One good friend took his father's rifle and killed himself on the day he was supposed to start university. The shock of that may have been part of why I took the path I did. As my own career unfolded – first as a teacher, youthworker, then psychologist and eventually worldwide campaigner for parents – it so often came back to the problems of being male. That seemed to be at the heart of much that was going wrong in the world.

I met Arne Rubinstein in the early days of the movement to change things for boys and men. My books *Manhood* and *Raising Boys* had struck a chord that resonated all over the world. It meant that I got to meet innovators and leaders and Arne was one of those who seemed to have real answers, along with the energy to put them into action.

In the 1990s, people were waking up to the fact that there was a male disaster happening, that men and boys were often unhappy and lost, and that something needed to be done. I knew there had to be a movement, because the problem was too large. A movement – like the civil rights movement, the women's movement, the trade union movement, the environment movement – happens when millions of people realise it's time for a change. It's an outbreak of commonsense. Arne's work with Rites of Passage for boys (and later girls too) was a pivotal aspect of helping our kids, and I was delighted to see it develop and unfold.

For our entire human history, a concerted effort has been needed to shift boys into good, strong and responsible men. This has been a preoccupation of every culture on earth. More than marriage, or funerals, or any other ritual, training boys to be men has been at the core of the community life of every society since the dawn of time.

People's lives have always depended on men being nurturing and life-protecting. And men themselves only thrive if they have a sense of purpose and an ethos for life.

Becoming a man is both a slow, and a rapid process. There is teaching from the moment a baby is born, in being loving, moderating but still standing with one's feelings, caring for others but respecting oneself, being alive and joyful, but safe. In adolescence, the teaching becomes more and more specific – handling vehicles, dealing with sexuality, making choices about work and career, responding to the choices offered around alcohol and drugs. Every parent is concerned about getting this right, but the tools have not always been there. Part of the genius of Arne's approach is to see that this is a community concern, and we have to build community with friends and family to help get each other's sons across the line. We must do this work together. It happens slowly, but it also comes to a climactic moment when a boy has to snap out of childishness and take hold of his life. Like giving birth, that moment needs lots of help.

No single father knows or has enough to provide his son with all he needs. No mother has enough to provide her daughter with all she needs. Together, as fathers, and as mothers, we have so much more strength and resources. It was the biggest mistake of the 20th century to think we can function alone. And the biggest relief, to start to band together around the goal of caring for our children and teens.

As you will read in this book, Arne's own story is quite remarkable. He has dedicated a lifetime to finding what will really help. He realised early on in his career as a doctor that it would take more than medication to solve the problems of society. He transformed his own life, and touched the lives of thousands of others in a beneficial way.

The Making of Men is written in the clearest language, full of great stories, and well organised to take you on a journey through the wonderful potential but also terrible hazards of being a boy. Arne has lived and worked up close with mothers and fathers of boys of all ages and stages and he shares what he has learned. So as you read *The Making of Men* it will be familiar ground, funny, encouraging, gritty and real. It will support you in organising how to help your son cross into manhood, and do so safely and with lifelong and transformative effects.

I really wish you well on this journey, which is an exciting one, and much better for having the clear road-map that this book provides.

Steve Biddulph
Adjunct Professor of Counselling
Cairnmillar Institute, Melbourne
Director, The Evandale Centre, Tasmania

PROLOGUE

It's just after 9 pm and I'm working in the Emergency Department of a regional Australian hospital. I graduated from medical school less than two months earlier and this is my first rotation. I'm only twenty-five.

An ambulance pulls up. I watch on the closed-circuit TV as the back door opens and a stretcher carrying a patient is carefully lifted out. The ambulance officer stops to speak with the head nurse and she points to a cubicle at the end of the ward. Behind the glass wall I watch as a handsome, well-dressed young man is wheeled past. He stares straight ahead. He has no obvious injuries.

The nurse comes in. 'Could be a real tragedy here, Dr Rubinstein,' she says. 'This kid took his dad's Mercedes for a joyride with two of his mates and they hit a telephone pole. He hasn't even got his licence yet – he's only sixteen. One of them has been airlifted to Melbourne in a critical condition and the other has a broken leg and chest injuries. This kid's only injury appears to be a seatbelt bruise. The ambulance guys say they smelled alcohol on his breath so we'll have to take a blood test. I know his family: his dad's a lawyer in town. He's going to kill him when he finds out.'

I pick up the chart and go and see the young man. He is okay apart from some scratches and a bruise on his chest. He tells me his name but says nothing else. He doesn't ask about his mates but I can see that he knows what has happened. His life is hanging in the balance. One or both of his mates could die and he might be going to jail. I can't stop wondering what made him do such a stupid thing.

• • •

Fast forward ten years and I'm working in the family practice that I own with another doctor. My last patient of the morning is Anne, a polite woman in her late thirties. Anne has been bringing her teenage son, Tom, to see me since he was little. I remember him as a fun, cheeky kid who loved thumb wrestling. I haven't seen him for a couple of years and suppose he must be about fifteen now.

Anne enters my office, slumps into the visitor's chair, and bursts into tears. 'I don't know what's happened to my beautiful boy,' she sobs. 'He's like a total stranger. He gets so angry for no reason and he shouts and throws things. I'm scared he's going to hit me. He spends all his time in his room playing some sort of online war game on his stupid computer. I'm really worried about what it's doing to his way of looking at the world. When he comes out of his room he's all jittery and I can't even talk to him; it's like he's about to explode.'

Anne tells me that her husband works long hours and when he is home he and Tom fight all the time. She pauses and I'm struck by her look of utter desperation.

'It's like I have two wild animals in the house which isn't big enough for both of them and they're competing with each other to be number one.' She lowers her voice. 'Sometimes I think they want to kill each other. Tom's started hanging out with a bad group of kids at school and my boy who is so clever failed half his exams this year. He used to tell me absolutely everything and now he won't even talk to me. He just gets so angry if I try to ask him what he's been doing.'

● ● ●

A few months ago I visited a close relative's nineteen-year-old son who was living at college while studying engineering. He was excited that I was coming to see him and when I arrived he took me around and introduced me to his mates. They were all doing different courses including international relations, law, economics and marketing. As well as studying hard, they played sport and were into either music or art or both. They always attended each other's performances on the field and on the stage.

These kids wanted to do something with their lives and saw this time at university as an important stepping stone. They were happy to chat and I found them engaging, interesting, and aware of the social issues that impact young people their age. They liked going out on the weekends and they drank a bit but they weren't into drugs. When they went to a party someone was always the designated driver to ensure everyone else got home safely. I felt they really supported and watched out for each other. They were so much more organised, clear and, dare I say it, well behaved than I was at that age!

• • •

As parents or carers, we try and give our kids a great start in life. We have such high hopes for them. So why do so many of them get into trouble as teenagers? Do you ever worry what will become of your son? Do you want to see him grow up to be happy, successful and excited about life? Why do some boys have such passion and make great choices while others go off the rails? Have you ever wondered how the enthusiastic, energetic kid who made you laugh, drove you nuts with questions, and had his fingers into everything, seemingly overnight turned into a grunting, monosyllabic teenager, unwilling or unable to communicate?

If these questions concern you, or if you've answered yes to any of them, this book is for you.

PART 1

WHAT'S HAPPENING TO OUR BOYS?

CHAPTER 1

Which way will your boy go?

Teenage boys are naturally loving, energetic, funny, creative and sensitive. They are passionate about the things that genuinely interest them, they are romantic and they are loyal. They love to laugh, can see the funny side of almost anything and can be both goofy and graceful at the same time. They have unlimited energy and can eat and eat as if they are dying of starvation, have a short break and then start eating again. Teenage boys sleep like the dead, grow taller in front of your very eyes and are always up for a wrestle. They are inspired and motivated and want to change the world. They are aware and have a strong sense of what is right and wrong, and they are brave and will do anything for something or someone they believe in.

I have also witnessed another side of teenage boys. I have seen anger that is violent, scary and cannot be reasoned with. I have seen deep, dark depression and I have known kids who believe the whole world is against them. Some have told me they don't care, that life sucks and that they hate everyone – including themselves. I have met talented boys who believe they are hopeless.

Most tragically of all, I have known boys who have chosen to end their lives.

Raising children is something most parents learn on the job. At the same time we have to work, pay the bills, care for others, and deal with everything else that is going on. What can *you* do to give your boy the best chance of becoming a happy and successful man? In fact, what can we as a society do to give *all* our boys the best chance to become happy and successful men?

The answers to these and other questions are what I want to share with you in this book. I want to give you an understanding of what is happening for your boy, the changes he is going through and the impact of things like technology on his world. Importantly, I want to explain in plain and simple terms what he needs from you as his parent or carer.

The Making of Men contains practical tips, techniques, exercises and strategies that will bring out the best in your son. I suggest ways you can help him avoid the dangers and issues that are part and parcel of being a teenager in the 21st century. And I show you exactly how to create what I believe is the critical missing link that our boys need – a properly run 'Rite of Passage' (ROP).

'Lift-off'

Think of your son as an astronaut. When he's young, our role as parents or carers is to help build him a rocket that will eventually carry him off on his own life journey. Naturally, we want him to have the greatest rocket possible, so we protect him, we feed him, we give him the best education we can and we love him unconditionally. Until he reaches puberty, we are in charge – more or less.

Somewhere between the ages of eleven and fifteen what I call 'lift-off' occurs. All of a sudden your boy and his rocket fire up on their own, there are a lot of flames and smoke and before we know it he has launched into … well *somewhere* … and it's certainly different from where he was before. At least physically, your son has begun to change from a boy to a man.

It is a well-documented fact that lift-off is the most dangerous stage for rockets. It's when they can head off course or even explode and come crashing back to earth. Most parents or carers would agree lift-off is also the most out-of-control time in their son's life. Many feel they have to either confront an enormous and explosive force, or sit back, watch the unfolding drama and hope and pray the outcome is okay. Lift-off is also unfortunately the time about which we seem to get the least education, the least support and have the least ability to influence what is happening.

It doesn't need to be like this. For thousands of years, societies around the world have believed that a boy's

3

entire future was determined by how well he and his family managed lift-off. In order to acknowledge and support their boys at this critical stage, these societies created structured and elaborate Rites of Passage. After all, this is the most important time in a male's life. It's when a boy needs to change not only *physically* but *psychologically* too. It's when he needs support and understanding not only from his parents but from the wider community. And he cannot do it on his own.

These days, we manage lift-off anywhere from poorly to not at all. I believe we have the ability to change this. I think it is possible for us to support the health and wellbeing of our young men at this crucial time. A lot of this book is about lift-off and the years immediately afterwards. If you can help your son to lift-off well then he'll have a great start to his adult life. If lift-off goes wrong then he may spend years dealing with the consequences.

What happens after lift-off?

Lift-off is generally over by the mid-teenage years. However, the period following can be difficult because your son wants to fly solo, though he's still well within earth's (meaning your) gravitational pull. At this point there can be a lot of disagreement about who is actually in control of the rocket. Your son may feel that it's his rocket and he should be able to fly it however and wherever he wants. You might think it's important you retain control of the rocket and that your son is not really responsible enough to be flying on his own ... yet. Radio communication may become strained. At times the radio may even get switched off completely. Occasionally, your young astronaut will find himself hungry or broke and will want to come back and land right in the middle of your kitchen table!

Eventually, he'll get to a point where he leaves the earth's gravitational pull and is out in space. Now he really *is* flying his rocket by himself. This stage can happen anywhere between the ages of seventeen and thirty-five – or even older. Ideally, it won't take that long. We hope that we have radio communication from here on in but it is certainly not a given. We hope our astronaut has all the necessary skills to fly his rocket, that he has some idea where he wants to go and that he knows we are there if he needs us. Our role as parents or carers has changed yet again. We can still offer support and love but now he has to fly solo.

Our job is to get our son to the stage where he leaves the earth's orbit and has everything he needs in order to navigate his own life journey in the best way possible.

Happiness and success

I hear so many people say they want their children to be happy and successful when they grow up, but when I ask them what that means they're often unsure. It's not surprising: I think our modern-day definitions of happiness and success are inappropriate and need to be challenged. Too often we measure these qualities in terms of what a person *does* or *has* compared to others – what sort of job he or she has or what material possessions he or she has acquired. According to our current definition, or at least what we see on TV and in the media, to be a successful man you have to be incredibly rich, surrounded by beautiful women, own a big house and drive an expensive car. It matters far less what sort of man you are and whether you do good things and maintain quality relationships.

Let's look at happiness and success another way. The word 'happy' is derived from the word 'happening'. So to be happy literally means to be *in what is happening*. In other words, to be happy is to be aware of and feeling whatever is happening *right now*. It's not about simply having a smile on your face, it's about genuinely experiencing what is going on around you.

How many times have you heard someone say they were at a wedding and they didn't feel happy, or they were at a funeral and they didn't feel sad? How many times have you been talking to someone and realised either they or you are not *fully* present in the conversation? Have you ever been somewhere beautiful, or at a great party, or with old friends, only to feel like you are not *really* there because your mind has drifted off? When this occurs you are not *in what is happening* and you are missing out on all that life has to offer.

> When I was working full-time as a doctor, even though it was often very busy, if I shut the door and focused one hundred per cent on my patient I found I enjoyed what I was doing and could cope with pretty much anything. If however, I was thinking about other things, worrying about this or that, rushing because I had something else to do, then I would feel stressed. I would get a dull headache and would find it hard to concentrate on what my patient was telling me.

The Power of Now by the German/Canadian writer Eckhart Tolle has sold millions of copies around the world and is one of the bestselling personal development books of all time. Tolle's message is simple. He suggests the secret to happiness and wellbeing is to be *present*, to be in the *now*, and to truly feel what is happening. When you're fully in the moment, you're more likely to cry tears of joy at a wedding or tears of sadness at a funeral. Life is not just about having a good time, it's about experiencing all of it, the good and the bad, the easy and the difficult, but most importantly, experiencing it when it actually *happens*.

Having enough money to look after ourselves and our families is important, but research has proven time that beyond a certain point, having *more* money and *more* possessions *doesn't* make you any happier. Still the message we receive is that we need more and more.

The belief that success is dependent on what you do or what you own has not served us well. Imagine instead if we defined success as having a great family, a rewarding job, being healthy and doing good in the community. Not everybody can be mega rich. In fact, most people never will be and it is unreasonable to strive for this. However, everyone *can* find a fulfilling and meaningful life through family, work, health and community.

If the message we give our sons is that they will only be happy and successful if they are rich (and famous) then we are setting them up for major problems. If the message we give them is that they can be happy and successful if they have good relationships and do something meaningful with their lives, then the outcome and what they aim to achieve will be very different.

My journey

The Making of Men is the result of a journey of more than thirty years working with boys and men as a doctor, coach, counsellor, mentor and facilitator of Rites of Passage (ROP) programs. When I was eighteen I had the privilege of living for six months in Jerusalem at the International Institute for Young Leaders. After that, I spent another six months living and working with a group of teenagers from all around the world. I knew at that stage I wanted to work with young people but it would take another dozen years to work out the best way to do that.

When I got back to Australia, I ran weekly groups for twelve- to sixteen-year-olds for three years and organised camping trips for them twice a year. It was an amazing experience and I got to see just how wonderful teenagers can be when given the right support. I also started my training to become a doctor and graduated at the age of twenty-five.

In 2001, after twelve years working in family practice and emergency medicine – and now with two young boys of my own – I made a major life and career change. In my spare time I'd been studying Rites of Passage in societies all over the world. I'd also been running camps for teenagers incorporating these techniques. The positive effects of these programs were incredible and the deeper I looked the more I could see how beneficial they were not only for the boys but also their families and their communities. I perceived a bottomless pit of need which I felt compelled to address. It started to take over my life but I knew in my heart that this was what I was supposed to be doing. I was also getting increasingly frustrated with the medical world and its emphasis on making money, not to mention the influence of the pharmaceutical companies. So at the age of thirty-seven I left my medical practice, which was just starting to become successful. I decided to go full-time into creating Rites of Passage programs and to find ways to train others so that we could run these programs around the country.

I believed then – and still believe today – that I am a

doctor. The difference is now I specialise in *preventative medicine*. This work helps boys (and girls) live happy and successful lives. It also has a positive benefit on their families, communities and people they work with. Since making this life change I have been a whole lot worse off financially, but my life has never felt richer or more fulfilled. It is definitely the best thing I ever did.

The big change that all boys go through

When I worked as a doctor it always amazed me how young boys – let's say those under eleven years of age – were so full of energy, loved to laugh and were so much fun. They were definitely some of my favourite patients. However, somewhere around the age of twelve to fourteen they all hit puberty – and that's when everything changes. For a good number of them, it's like a switch is flipped. They stop communicating, they start wearing caps or hoodies, they slouch around like they're about to fall over, and they generally look miserable.

There are other boys the same age who are doing really well. They have interests and hobbies, like music or sport. They may not know what they want to do when they're older, but they know they want to do *something*. They have good friends and they're happy to talk about what is going on in their world. These kids are motivated and inspired. They are hungry for opportunities to pursue all that life has to offer.

Having given talks and seminars to thousands of

parents across all demographics of wealth and geography, I know that many feel as if they are in a sort of lottery with their boys. They love them dearly and want them to be happy, safe and successful, but they fear their sons will succumb to the many dangers and pressures of modern life.

A lottery is about luck and I no longer believe that how our boys turn out is purely a matter of luck. There are key elements that influence how your son will get on as a teenager and whether or not he will develop into a happy and successful adult. In this book I will identify those key elements and explain what you as a parent or carer need to do.

Our aim is to support our teenagers so they continue to be all those great things I mentioned at the start of this chapter. *The Making of Men* is about maximising the wonderful side of this time in their lives. I promise you: teenage boys being wonderful is not just wishful thinking or empty words, it is actually their natural state.

Modern families

I am a father with two sons who are now in their twenties. Their mother and I separated and divorced when they were young. I love my sons with all my heart and am proud of the young men they have become but I was by no means the perfect dad and I made plenty of mistakes. My sons will definitely confirm this! Looking back I can see that there are some things that I did well and other things that I would now do differently. I wish I had prioritised them more over my work. I wish I had really listened to them instead of being distracted so often. I wish I had lost my temper less and I wish that I had taken a more active interest in what was happening for them at school.

Like most parents, I was learning on the job. It would have been great if there had been a different sort of parent support back then. A way of knowing what my boys' needs were at different times in their lives – apart from the obvious cravings for mountains of food and endless sleep! I would have loved to have had more people to talk to and get advice from and it would have been helpful if I had been open to listening and receiving advice. It would have been great to have had this book.

These days, families are infinitely complex. There is the so-called 'normal' family that has been statistically proven to consist of mum and dad living together with their 2.4 children. But there are also families with single mums or single dads. There are same-sex families where two women or two men are bringing up the kids. There are families where one parent has died. There are families with only one child and others with more than ten. And as we know, every single person and every single family is different. Whatever your family structure, whatever your specific parenting arrangements, this book will be of help to you.

What about girls?

The Making of Men is about boys and men, however much of it is just as relevant to girls. Teenage girls are naturally wonderful and gorgeous but many of them have just as tough a time during adolescence. Issues such as self-harm, mental illness and precocious sexual behaviour are on the rise. Whether you have a son or a daughter you will find this book of value.

How to use this book

The Making of Men is all about what we can do to bring out the best in our kids. It is about solutions. It is not about identifying and then wallowing in the problems. I want to show you exactly what you can do in order to support your young man both as a teenager and later in life. We need to know what is going on and we need to be able to name the dangers. I will do this in the first few chapters and I recommend that you read them carefully as you may well be enlightened.

I hope you relate to my ideas and the real-life stories in this book. It may be like a light bulb has been switched on. Naturally, you may disagree with some of the things I have to say. *The Making of Men* will likely make you reassess your own childhood. Some of you will feel happy and lucky about the way you were brought up and others will feel that your childhood experiences left a lot to be desired. Remember, we are all in this together and the aim of this book is to pass on knowledge so that you don't have to try and work it all out yourself. Life in the 21st century is challenging and exciting and there is so much going on that our kids need help to find their own personal success and avoid the pitfalls. They are the future and we have a responsibility to give them the best kickstart that we possibly can.

Key Points from Chapter 1

- Teenage boys are naturally loving, happy and motivated

- There are many potential issues facing our young men – from drugs, to peer group pressure and the influence of technology

- Happiness and success should be defined by having good relationships and doing something meaningful, not by how much money or how many possessions you have

CHAPTER 2

The biggest transition of all: from boy to man

Steve, a forty-four-year-old computer technician says, 'No one ever taught me how to be a man. I grew up believing that a real man was big and strong, could drink lots of beer, had all the pretty girls after him and was great at football ... oh, and of course he didn't cry. Real men were tough, weren't afraid to get in fights, didn't show their emotions and always knew what they were doing.

'I became depressed as a teenager. I wasn't very big or strong, I didn't like beer, I was shy with girls, not very good at football, afraid of fights, still cried sometimes when I was sad and definitely didn't know what I was doing with my life. I thought there was something seriously wrong with me.'

Moving from being a boy to a young man is the greatest change in the life of any male. His body will alter automatically and dramatically when he goes through puberty and over a period of twelve or so months he will physically transform in every way. At the same time how he sees himself and how he thinks about himself, how he views the world and how the world views him, must also change in equal measure.

The differences between a boy and a man

If you line up a group of a teenagers (or even adult men) you won't be able to tell by looking at them who is a man and who is still a boy. It is possible still to be a boy but in a man's body (just ask any woman!). Being a man is about where your mind is at – not how big or strong you are. In order to become a man, there needs to be a psychological shift in the way you think, see yourself and see those around you. For some men this shift will happen quickly, for some it will happen over a period of years and for some it may never happen at all. The quicker and more fully the psychological shift happens once a boy reaches puberty the better and the greater the impact on his health and wellbeing. The longer it takes and the more it is avoided or denied, the bigger the potential problems.

Young boys believe they are the centre of the universe. They are always wanting acknowledgement and they need constant mothering. Men, on the other hand, know that they are part of a family and community which they need to support, they do things because they believe they are right and they seek genuine relationships rather than mothering.

A boy trapped in a man's body

When a man has a temper tantrum if he doesn't get what he wants; looks to his wife or partner for mothering; refuses to take responsibility for his actions or seeks to blame others; bullies those who work for him; refuses to listen to another's opinion; needs power and constant acknowledgement to feel okay about himself … these are all instances of men behaving like boys.

A boy who has made the psychological shift into 'man psychology' will find the world a much easier place in which to live. Boy psychology is concerned with being number one, needing to have everything you want – regardless of whether you even need it – and needing to have it right now. Boy psychology in men is often selfish and frequently ignores the needs of others. Boy psychology can be destructive and abusive.

Of course, boy psychology in a boy is acceptable and normal. Children ought to behave like children, not adults. But boy psychology in a man is not good for anyone, even though in our culture aspects of boy psychology are often presented as something to aspire to. They're not. Having boys in positions of power is potentially disastrous, as they are likely to think more about what they want for themselves rather than what is best for their community.

Boy or man?

The table below outlines the six main differences I have identified between boy psychology and healthy man psychology:

Boy Psychology	Healthy Man Psychology
I am the centre of the universe and I need constant acknowledgement	I am part of the universe and I do what I believe is right
Other males are competition and power is for me	I work together with other men and power is for the good of the community
I will live forever	I am mortal and will die one day
I take no responsibility for my actions	I take full responsibility for my actions
I am ruled by my emotions	I can stand with my emotions
I want a mother	I seek a relationship with the feminine

The boy psychology factors above are what you would typically see in an eight-year-old. These behaviours are normal, they are acceptable and there is nothing inherently wrong with them. We want eight-year-olds to be boys, we don't want them to be men. But we need eighteen- and forty-year-olds to be men rather than boys. Let's look at each of the factors one by one.

Boy: 'I am the centre of the universe and I need constant acknowledgement'

Young boys believe the whole world revolves around them. They mostly think about themselves, they only want to do what they want, and more often than not they are blind to what is going on for others. This is normal boy psychology. Young boys have an insatiable need to be seen and acknowledged. 'Look at me, Mummy, look at me!' 'Watch me kick the football, watch me jump!' 'Listen to me sing this song!' 'Look at what I made at school today!' They will do anything for attention and constantly want to be told how wonderful they are.

Many parents, especially mums, adore watching their boys and derive enormous joy from even the smallest achievement. They are happy to continually tell them how wonderful they are. While needing to be seen and constantly acknowledged is normal in a young boy, it is neither healthy nor attractive in a man.

June is forty. 'I don't believe my son thinks I even exist once I drop him off at school. I work hard all day and when he comes home I ask him all about his day but he never asks me about mine. I don't mind that my son is like that but it drives me mad that my husband is exactly the same.'

Men operating on boy psychology are often self-centred. They tend to think that everything in the world is there just for them. They may come home from work and expect dinner to be ready and then want to sit and watch TV or read the paper instead of lending a hand. They may want their wife or partner to always be telling them how great they are and they can be selfish in putting their own needs first without thinking about other members of the family. At work, men operating on boy psychology are the ones who always have to have it their own way and are not prepared to listen to others' ideas. They are selfish and believe that they and their needs are more important than everybody else's.

Healthy man: 'I am part of the universe and I do what I believe is right'

A healthy man recognises that the world doesn't revolve around him and that he is in fact part of something much larger. This knowledge influences how he relates to other people and events, and his ability to recognise the feelings and needs of others. He realises that he is connected to what is happening around him and that his actions have greater consequences than simply how they affect him personally.

A healthy man has a sense of purpose and does something because he believes in it, because it is the right thing to do, and because he knows it. Being seen and acknowledged for his achievements or making lots of money are not the driving reasons behind his actions. Instead, the motivation to act comes from a deeper place in which he knows that it is the right action for him to take – for the greater good.

Boy: 'Other males are competition and power is for me'

Most boys see other boys as competition. They will wrestle, have running races, throw balls as far as they can, play games, and do anything to try and see who is number one. They reluctantly share and will look after themselves without worrying about those around them. Have you ever given your son a chocolate bar or some sort of treat and watched him eat it in front of you without offering you any?

This boy behaviour is seen in many men today. Competitive urges drive these overgrown boys relentlessly as they seek to beat the next man by acquiring more money or possessions. The global financial crisis and the greed of many in the banking industry is an example of boy psychology at its worst. The few with power don't care about the millions who are affected by their actions and lose their jobs, houses and life savings. They are blinded by the power that money represents for them and they just want more.

Many men today who make vast sums of money use it to build bigger houses, buy more luxurious cars and take increasingly expensive holidays, rather than looking to see how much good they could be doing in the world. These same men are often working longer and longer hours, spending less time with their families and are driven to make more and more money, even though they don't really need it and don't derive genuine satisfaction from it.

Healthy man: 'I work together with other men and power is for the good of the community'

A healthy man thinks about power in a different way. He doesn't see other men as purely competition and looks for ways they can support each other and work together towards common goals. While boy psychology separates men and sets them against each other, men operating on healthy man psychology recognise that their true power lies in working as a team. They use their power to protect and support those around them, their families and their community, and work towards a future they believe in.

Philanthropists recognise they have more money than they personally need and spend their time helping others. Some of the world's wealthiest men, people like Bill Gates and Warren Buffet, are giving away large parts of their fortunes. They are supporting projects like the eradication of serious diseases and providing safe drinking water to people in third world countries. In Australia, men like Dick Smith, Michael Traill and Daniel Petre have changed their careers from ones where they were making high incomes to ones where they focus on creating positive outcomes in society.

It is not only those with large amounts of money who benefit their communities; there are thousands of men who work as volunteers in organisations like Rotary, Apex and Lions Club, to name just a few. These men give their time, raise funds and support those in society who are disadvantaged. They acknowledge they have enough spare time and energy to be able to help others and they do so. Many of them do this anonymously and are motivated by how much they can give to the world, rather than how much they can get from it.

Boy: 'I will live forever'

A young boy does not think that he will die. He believes that he is immortal and that the world wouldn't exist if he wasn't there. You only have to watch boys playing to see how many of their games involve joyfully shooting and killing each other to realise that they have little idea what death is really about. This belief is normal for a young boy. We don't need or want young children to be too aware of their mortality. Those who witness death and tragic events can be left with deep emotional scars that can take a lifetime to heal.

In men, the boyish feeling of invincibility can result in risk-taking behaviour with potentially disastrous consequences. The greatest numbers of road deaths involve young men under the age of twenty-five. Speed is almost always a factor. These young men believe that they are indestructible and that they can drive as fast as they want without understanding the true risks.

Another way this boy psychology is demonstrated in men is when they eat badly and excessively, drink heavily and/or take drugs. There is an attitude that 'my body can cope', 'I will be young forever' and 'I don't have a problem'. You only have to look at them to know that in fact they do.

Healthy man: 'I am mortal and will die one day'

A healthy man knows he will not live forever. This knowledge influences how he conducts himself and the decisions he makes. I remember a friend of mine saying that he didn't want to be seventy-four and look back with the realisation that he hadn't done what he wanted to and now it was too late. Understanding our mortality helps us to appreciate our own life and what we do with it, as well as understanding how precious a gift it is. A big part of my decision to leave my medical practice came from my belief that I wanted to live my life to the fullest and that helping kids is what I believe I am supposed to be doing. I knew that I didn't want to spend my entire career working as a doctor even though I had spent so many years studying.

Healthy man psychology doesn't mean you don't do stuff that may be dangerous or challenging. It just means that you think about them first, you plan and you try and avoid truly reckless or stupid things.

Boy: 'I take no responsibility for my actions'

It is a natural reaction in a child to avoid responsibility and shift the blame when something goes wrong. One boy I knew threw a ball and broke a window. I watched him try to explain to his father how it wasn't his fault because he had tripped while he was running and the ball had just 'accidentally jumped out of his hand'. Another common scenario is when a boy's team loses at sport and he blames the umpire. 'If he'd given us a fair go instead of favouring the other team we would have won!'

We don't have to look much further than politics to see boy psychology operating in grown men. It often seems the standard way to deal with a mistake is to blame someone else, cover it up or deny it. We have become so used to this we accept it as normal.

Of course, this sort of behaviour is not confined to politics and happens in many homes and workplaces. At work, a boss operating on boy psychology will blame and even fire members of his team when something doesn't pan out rather than taking responsibility for what is his job and what he is paid for. At home, some men fear their wives or children seeing them as anything but perfect. Like a child, they will avoid responsibility by making excuses and shifting blame. Ask any woman how often her husband or partner will actually admit he has made a mistake or that he was wrong.

Healthy man: 'I take full responsibility for my actions'

A healthy man is prepared to take responsibility for his actions and their consequences – even if they are not what were intended.

I remember being in the car with my father when I was about twelve. He took a wrong turn down a quiet suburban street with a low speed limit. Realising his mistake he made a U-turn which was technically illegal. Suddenly a motorbike came speeding around the turn, skidded but couldn't stop in time and ran into us. The rider was catapulted over the top of our car and onto the road. My father, who was also a doctor, didn't hesitate. He leapt out and ran to help the rider who fortunately was okay. Dad helped him lift up his bike and together we walked him back to his house which happened to be around the corner. What struck me was that my father didn't try and make any excuses or claim that the rider was going too fast, as he almost certainly was. His concern was for the man's welfare. He stayed with him until he was safely home and he offered to pay in full for the damage to his bike. He could have simply left his phone number with the man and even gone to court to avoid paying for everything but my father took full responsibility there and then for his actions and what happened as a result.

Boy: 'I am ruled by my emotions'

Young boys tend to give their emotions free rein. When a five-year-old is not allowed to have an ice cream or is told to turn off the TV and go to bed, chances are he'll lose his temper. He might even have a tantrum and tell you he doesn't love you and that you are the worst parent in the world! Most of us have witnessed this sort of behaviour and we just hope they grow out of it sooner rather than later.

While it may be unpleasant and upsetting when a young boy loses his temper, if the same thing happens in a man it is a very different issue. A man who cannot handle his emotions and becomes physically or verbally abusive when he doesn't get what he wants is behaving in a way that is unacceptable, and possibly criminal. Domestic violence is a tragic indication of the inability of many men to keep their emotions in check.

At work, boy psychology makes men think they are allowed to shout at people and to shame them. I remember as a young doctor helping one of the senior surgeons in an operation. I noticed how attentive and polite all the nurses were and how hard they worked to make sure the surgeon had everything that he wanted. In retrospect, I realised they were terrified of him. It was a long and stressful operation but all went to plan. Towards the end, one of the nurses dropped an instrument on the floor. It made no difference to the operation but it just meant that we had to wait a few minutes while she went to get a steri-lised replacement.

To my horror the surgeon lost his temper. He started swearing and yelling at the poor nurse who looked shattered. He was just like a child having a temper tantrum. He threw a tray of instruments across the room – all because he was going to have to wait five minutes longer to finish and go for his lunch break.

Healthy man: 'I can stand with my emotions'

A healthy man has to be able to handle what cards he is dealt and find ways other than anger, blame, denial, emotional outbursts and violence to resolve issues.

I remember a patient of mine who had separated from his wife and was very angry about what had happened. Crucially, though, he was able to admit that he was angry, that he didn't like that he felt that way, and that is why he had sought help. He said to me, 'I know if I do get angry and tell her what I think it may make me feel better for a few minutes but it could actually end up really ugly. It certainly isn't going to do my kids any good. I think it'd be better if I went to the gym instead and came and talked to you. I know I'm also responsible for what's happened and if I can work on that then maybe I won't feel angry any more.'

To his credit, this man found other ways to deal with his anger, was able to maintain a good relationship with his children, and has now been to mediation with his wife.

Boy: 'I want a mother'

Young boys want their mums to tidy their rooms, pick up their clothes, cook their food and tell them how wonderful they are. All the time. They want their mothers to help them up when they fall over, dust them off, tend to their wounds, give them a kiss and send them back out to play. Young boys want their mothers to always be available for affection and to think about the boy's needs before their own.

While most mums are only too happy to do everything their boys need and want, many women have told me that the grown men they know or have married are *still* seeking a mother ... and there are very few women who want to mother men, especially when they have children of their own!

Healthy man: 'I seek a relationship with the feminine'

A healthy man relates to the feminine with respect and embraces the fullness of nurturing, passion, protection and creation. This way of relating can take many forms and is different from seeking a mother or treating women as merely sex objects. Relating to the feminine is not just about sleeping with a woman. It is a journey that involves appreciating the beautiful things that are all around us, the wonder of creation, the magnificence of nature, the insights of coincidence and the highs and lows of passion.

Of course, not all men express their relationship to the feminine by actually being with a woman. Men can

29

recognise and find beauty, nurturing, creativity, respect and passion in other ways. It may be through art, it may be with motorbikes or cars, it may be with nature, or it may be with another man. How well a man expresses his relationship to the feminine is a big part of his life that directly impacts on his happiness and wellbeing.

Men **know** when they are acting like boys (they really do)

One of the basic differences between a boy and a man is that a boy is largely unaware of his behaviour and therefore has little choice in what he does. As grown men, on the other hand, we can tell when we are in boy psychology and when we are in healthy man psychology.

I would love to be able to say that at my age and with all the work I have done that I always operate within healthy man psychology. It would be great to know that I never do things for acknowledgement, I readily share power, I take full responsibility for my actions, I am aware of my mortality, and I never look to my partner for mothering. Unfortunately, it is simply not true and probably more often than I care to admit I am guilty of all of these boy psychology behaviours. In fact, I can see myself moving between boy and man psychology and I definitely know if I stop and think about it at any moment which one I am in.

My aim is to spend less and less time in boy psychology and more time in healthy man psychology. Because

I'm aware of which state I'm in, I also have a choice. I can do things as a boy or as a man. I cannot blame others; nor can I make excuses.

I know when I do something within boy psychology, like for example not admitting at work when I have made a mistake and getting defensive about my actions. I can find myself making excuses and even defending something I know is wrong. Naturally, my colleagues feel disappointed or even angry when I do this and for a time it affects how we are working together. Fortunately, I work in an environment where we are usually able to call each other out on these sorts of behaviours.

When I am in healthy man psychology, it supports other healthy man psychology actions and events. For example, when my son came to visit recently he really wanted to spend time just with me. At first I said that I couldn't take time off as I was too busy. He said that it was important, so I cancelled what I was doing and we spent a couple of days together. We had a really fun time and were able to have some great conversations that ended up in him asking me for advice regarding something that had been worrying him. It created the opportunity for me to be able to support him in his life.

A world running on boy psychology looks like ...

It's a sad fact that modern society frequently validates and even champions boy psychology. Our definition of success is often based on boy psychology rather than healthy man psychology. We live in an age where the superheroes are not those who do the most good, but those who have accumulated the most money and possessions. We rarely honour the man who works hard to support his family and be a great father; instead we make TV shows about the lives of the super rich and famous ... and often super egotistical. We rarely acknowledge men who work tirelessly for their communities; instead we make ads that suggest success is defined by the car you drive or how pretty your girlfriend is. We rarely praise the sportsmen who do their personal best times; we are only interested in the winners who can beat everybody else. If you come second then you are considered the first of the losers even if you have swum or run faster than ever before.

While boy psychology can be great for TV ratings and selling luxury goods, it simply does not work for young men. Once boys reach puberty things *must* change. If young men are still seeking continual acknowledgement, still wanting to be the centre of the universe, still shirking responsibility, still throwing tantrums when they don't get what they want, and still looking to be mothered, they are going to struggle in life. It can be a rude awakening when all of a sudden no one thinks you're cute any more, people stop telling you how wonderful you are just because you can do up your shoelaces and you have to start looking after yourself.

When we fail to acknowledge and support the psychological transition from boy to man, confusion, anger and eventually depression can result.

Women are more aware than men of the need for change and the consequences are reflected in the divorce rate. Over fifty per cent of marriages in Australia now end in divorce, with four out of five being initiated by women. I have spoken to countless women who tell me that they don't want to be married to a boy, they don't want to mother their husband, and they are no longer prepared to keep putting up with having a child for a partner.

Boy psychology in society

When I think about our leaders today, the ones that we elect and the ones in positions of power at work and within our communities, I wonder how many of them have a true vision, as opposed to doing just about anything they can to hold onto their power. How many of them act with the long-term consequences in mind rather than taking short-term actions that will make them look good now but will create greater problems down the track? Do our leaders truly take responsibility for their actions, or do they blame others and make excuses? Do they treat the environment and our natural resources as precious and deserving of preservation, or do they treat them as never-ending supplies, with pollution and global warming just being an unavoidable consequence?

Imagine if all our leaders functioned within healthy man psychology. Imagine if we had leaders who were visionaries who sought to improve the health and well-being of all humankind; leaders who thought about the consequences of their actions and how they would impact future generations; leaders who were prepared to hand over power when the time was right, and who treated the earth and the environment as something to improve over time rather than ignore and pillage.

A society that runs on boy psychology will act as if the earth is an unlimited resource, or that the effects of human behaviour don't matter as the problems won't affect our generation. This society will accept the decimation of forests, pour unlimited amounts of greenhouse gases and toxins into the atmosphere, and allow the rivers and oceans to become polluted. The future success, happiness and sustainability of our world depends on men acting in ways that are based on healthy man psychology rather than on boy psychology.

Unrecognised and unchecked boy psychology leads a man to believe that material possessions and power over others are what defines him as successful. This allows him to ignore the consequences of his actions and often has a disastrous effect on his relationships with women and at a societal level with the earth we live on. This needs to be recognised and dealt with.

How we can help our sons move from boy psychology to healthy man psychology

Christian is twenty-one. 'I hated becoming a teenager. My body changed quickly and I grew over 30 centimetres in a year. All of a sudden I was bigger than the rest of my family and none of my clothes fitted me. I felt really awkward, I kept bumping into things and I was uncoordinated. I had to start shaving and wear lots of deodorant or else I stank. I also had lots of pimples. I was really tall and people kept telling me I was a man now but I sure didn't feel like one. Mum still treated me like a baby and Dad still bossed me around. It was a confusing time. I had lots of new thoughts in my head but no one to talk to. I remember feeling anxious and I didn't even want to leave my room. It took me over three years to start to relax again and feel comfortable about who I was. I wish it had happened a lot quicker, they were my hell years.'

We as parents and carers need to do something that can create and support the transition our boys so badly need. If we don't, then they risk becoming stuck in the worst place of all – somewhere between a boy and a man but not fitting properly into either.

Christian's story is a classic case of 'extended adolescence'. This condition can last for years or even decades. You only have to look at young teenagers to see how awkward and uncomfortable a place adolescence can be. They are no longer boys, as evidenced by the physical changes, but they are not yet men. They are lost without guidance in an in-between place where the world as they know it has broken down but they have not yet discovered a new reality that makes sense to them. Extended adolescence is a bad place to be and can lead to anxiety, depression, anger and withdrawal. What is needed is a process that helps the teenager get through this stage, and ensures he doesn't get stuck there.

This problem is not a new or modern one. Indigenous societies and communities around the world recognised thousands of years ago that something had to be done to help this transition happen at the right time in a boy's life. They developed elaborate Rites of Passage (ROP) where the boys going through puberty would be separated from the rest of the tribe. They would undergo an initiation ritual to become young men. These ancient societies considered it to be the most important thing that they could do for their boys.

There are tribes and communities in Africa, Australia and Papua New Guinea that have never had any physical contact with one another. The only thing they have in common is the knowledge they accumulated after observing the behaviour of men and boys over countless generations. They all came to the same conclusion

– boys need some sort of Rite of Passage in order to become young men. Our modern culture is the first in the history of humankind that has dispensed with this essential tradition. It is really no surprise that we find ourselves in a world that is dominated by boy psychology.

In the next chapter we'll take a look at exactly why boys behave badly. We'll also examine the enormous challenges they face in today's complex modern world.

Key Points from Chapter 2

- Boys believe they are the centre of the universe and want mothering

- Men know they are part of a community and want relationships

- Boy psychology in men is destructive to our world

- The move to healthy man psychology is vital and is helped by a Rite of Passage (ROP)

CHAPTER 3

Why boys muck up

Five-year-old Simon was a fun little guy who came to my medical centre when he had a cold or fell of his bike. One time he used the sole of his foot as a brake on the front wheel of his bike and wore the skin right off his foot. He still has the scar to prove it.

Simon always visited with his mum. One day his mum told me she was worried as he had started wetting his bed again after nearly two years. He was also having temper tantrums. He was not sick and his mum didn't know what to do.

I asked her if there was anything else going on. She told me that Simon's dad wasn't around. Some unpleasant stuff had happened between them years ago and they never heard from him again. She hadn't thought it was a problem but recently there had been a father's event at pre-school and while all the other kids had their dads there, Simon had no one to go with him. Ever since then he had been wetting his bed and losing his temper.

When a boy is not having his basic needs met, he will likely behave in a way that is not ideal, beautiful or loving. It's actually no different whatever age you are. In the case of a young man, if he's withdrawn or angry or always getting in trouble, it is not because he is bad or dumb, it means something else is going on. Maybe he feels he is not being seen, no one knows who he really is or he feels like he has to put on an act. Maybe he is uncertain about what he is supposed to be doing with his life, maybe he wants to talk to girls but doesn't feel comfortable doing so, maybe he and his dad fight all the time and his dad makes him feel small …

The good news is that it is usually possible to work out the cause. The most important thing is to be aware and have a healthy relationship, which includes good communication, so that it becomes clear. How to deal with the issue and who is the best person to support the boy or young man will vary. Sometimes they need their mum, sometimes their dad, sometimes someone outside of the immediate family. However, there is always a way to help them improve the situation.

The needs of a boy are different from those of a young man. Boys look to us to fix things. We can tell them what to do, or change something for them to make it all right. Boys believe what we say, and our help and love makes a big difference to their health and wellbeing. Young men, on the other hand, have to work it out themselves and decide how they are going to deal with whatever situations arise. We can support them in many ways but in the end it is up to them. They have to move from a place where they feel like a victim – the 'Why is this happening to me?' mentality – to one where they accept what's going on and then look for ways to best cope with it and get on with it.

In young Simon's case there is no perfect solution. Thankfully, his mother was able to talk to him and tell him that even though his father didn't live with them he still loved him. She arranged for Simon to spend some time with an uncle who made a big fuss of him and took him skateboarding and bike riding. After a couple of months Simon stopped wetting his bed and his temper tantrums settled.

I spent time working with Simon years later when he was a teenager. He was angry and getting into all sorts of trouble including experimenting with drugs and binge drinking. He came on one of our programs and there he had the opportunity to listen to other men who had grown up without fathers talk about how it had been for them. The realisation that he was not the only one and that other men got through it and were able to move on with their lives had a massive impact. One man talked about how when he became a dad, not having had a father himself, he made a promise that he would always take an active part in his son's upbringing. He said he tried as hard as he could to be the best father possible for his boy. He took him to school most days, was home for dinner at night and went to all of his boy's sporting events.

We also gave Simon the chance to talk about how he felt not having a dad. This experience didn't make up for the fact that Simon had no father in his life, but it did give him hope, as well as the ability to take control of his situation.

To this day I still see Simon. He is a great young man who now works in the hospitality industry. He loves his music and he loves to party but he doesn't do drugs and he hardly ever drinks. He is not yet a father but he talks about it and I know that one day some kid is going to be really lucky to have him as their dad.

The physical, emotional and spiritual roller coaster

At the onset of puberty, which is usually between the ages of eleven and fourteen, a boy experiences enormous changes physically, emotionally and spiritually.

Physically, he will have a massive increase in the circulating levels of testosterone which will lead in a period of just a few months to:

1. The appearance of pubic hair on his genitals and his armpits

2. A growth spurt which can be upwards of 30 cm in twelve months
3. Deepening of his voice
4. The growth of his testicles and the lengthening and thickening of his penis
5. Hair growing on his face
6. An increase in muscle mass leading to an overall increase in strength and endurance.

Add to that the beginning of real sexual function which can be overwhelming and involve wet dreams, unwanted erections brought on at any time by almost anything and frequent urges to masturbate.

Peter is twenty-four. 'I was the first one in my class to start getting pubic hair. It was embarrassing especially as after sport and swimming we all showered together. I started wearing my underpants because I didn't want any of the other boys to tease me.

'I was growing so fast it was ridiculous. My clothes didn't fit and my jeans were way above my ankles. My hands and feet seemed enormous and I kept tripping over things. I felt totally awkward. My hair had become greasy and I started getting pimples. That horrified me and I would spend hours in front of the mirror squeezing them and checking on their progress. I felt completely ugly. To make matters worse, my voice was breaking and at times it would sound squeaky which I hated.

'At thirteen I started having wet dreams a couple of times a week. I used to put my sheets in the washing machine and not say a word to my mum. She never mentioned anything even though for a couple of years she had all my extra washing to do. All I knew is that when I came home my bed would be made and clean pyjamas would be under my pillow. I stopped going to friends' houses for sleep-overs as I was scared I'd have a wet dream and that would be a total disaster which I knew I would have no idea how to deal with.

'I would fantasise about anyone. A girl I knew, a woman I saw on television or in a movie, a porno magazine that I had found in a pile of newspapers outside someone's house. At one point I even started fantasising about boys and I thought maybe I was gay.

'Girls were just a nightmare. I was painfully shy and even though there were schoolgirls on the train that I really liked and wanted to talk to I was way too embarrassed to even try.

I would be totally lost for words or more often than not say something dumb or even worse be blushing bright red. They seemed so much more confident than me so I ended up just trying to hide somewhere away from everyone and pretended to be reading my book.

'It was a difficult time. I had no one to talk to. I didn't want to talk to Mum and Dad wasn't really available. I wouldn't have even known how to start the conversation. The other boys at school were no good to talk to. They all seemed to know what was going on and they used to boast about their sexual conquests. It seemed like I was the only one who was unsure about it all and not having sex. I later found out that for nearly all of them it was false bravado and they were making it up but at the time I believed it was true. I'm really glad that time in my life is over and I really wish it had been different.'

Emotionally, during puberty, your son will be trying to make sense of what is happening around him and work out his place in it all. How does he relate to his family, his peers and indeed to the world? What does he want to do with his life and is it a problem if he has absolutely no idea? What are these new feelings for girls (or boys)? What are these new ideas that seem to be consuming him?

Spiritually, he may wonder whether there is some higher power that has pre-determined his fate or whether he is a lone sailor on a sea filled with other lone sailors. As a boy, he would have been given the beliefs and ideologies of his school and his parents. Now as a young man he will question this. He may continue with those beliefs or he may decide to forge his own way of looking at the world.

All of this is challenging and confronting for a young man. As a boy, much of his life was laid out for him. He simply got out of bed in the morning and his day began. Boys don't really have a lot of say in what they do. Now all of a sudden he is either making more decisions or becoming very aware that others are wanting to make decisions for him.

A boy's brain continues to develop through puberty and MRI research has shown that higher-order brain centres, such as the pre-frontal cortex, don't fully develop until young adulthood. The pre-frontal cortex is the area of the brain responsible for reasoning and problem solving. In calm situations, young men can rationalise almost as well as adults, but under stress this ability can get hijacked and their decision-making can be irrational and unpredictable. The pre-frontal cortex also controls things like outbursts of anger and extreme emotions. This explains why teenagers so easily lose their tempers and under stress are likely to make decisions that really don't seem to make any sense at all ... except to them, of course.

Mental pressure

At some schools, boys as young as ten or eleven are already doing hours and hours of homework each night – and the expectations are that the volume just increases the older you get. Young men at high school who want to go on to tertiary education often have to start doing large amounts of homework three to four years before they leave school. They are under constant pressure to succeed and if they don't they risk not getting into their preferred course. Every year there are fewer university places than there are candidates so there is the ever-present threat of failure.

Years ago, if you dropped out of school you could bum around for a while and then go for an apprenticeship as a carpenter, plumber, boilermaker or tradesman and be fairly sure of an income. Today, apprenticeships are hard to come by and require applicants to have completed a school certificate or equivalent in order to be considered. If a young man leaves school and goes on social security benefits then his chances of completing any form of higher education or getting long-term meaningful employment start to rapidly decrease.

Pressure is not only present through academic demands at school. There is also peer group pressure on young men to look a certain way, to wear the right clothes, to have a girlfriend and to own the latest gadgets. Many young men simply do not naturally fit into the categories that others say they should and so feel pressured to either conform to something that isn't real for them, or to go their own way and risk rejection.

There is also peer group pressure to behave in ways which may not be in the best interests of the young man. Others may try to persuade him into acting cool or aloof with girls, even if he is not comfortable with this. There may be pressure to take drugs or drink when he doesn't want to. For a young man, at a time when acceptance is so important, this peer group pressure can be very difficult to resist.

The role of a parent or carer

Most parents or carers are aware of the challenges facing young people but the hardest thing is working out what we can do about it. What's certain is that it's too risky to expect our teenagers will just go through 'whatever it is they have to go through', completely alone, and then eventually pop out the other side as well-balanced, happy adults. The transition from boy to young man is the most difficult, significant and complex change our sons will experience and they need all the help they can get. What happens to young men during this period of transition will affect them for the rest of their lives. It will affect the choices they make, the relationships they form and the type of men they become.

Not only is this an issue for the young men themselves, there is an equal cost for the rest of society. These young men are the future parents, partners and leaders of our communities. We need them to be fully alive and able to contribute to society in the best way possible. We have a responsibility to be doing whatever we can to give them every opportunity to reach their full potential.

• • •

Research on thousands of people of all ages has shown that at twelve years of age the level of satisfaction with life or feeling of wellbeing is at its highest. This is not surprising given that in Australia most twelve-year-old boys have lots of great privileges and few if any responsibilities. They go to good schools, can play lots of sport, have computers, mobile gaming systems and mobile phones to communicate with their friends. They have lots of fun activities after school and on weekends and they don't have to worry about work or feeding themselves as their parents take care of all of that.

The Complementary Medicine Department at the Royal Melbourne Institute of Technology surveyed a wide range of people and produced the following graph which charts 'Subjective Wellbeing'. It shows that after peaking at twelve years of age a person's perception of their wellbeing plummets dramatically until by the age of sixteen a person's level of satisfaction with life is actually at its *lowest*.

This rapid drop occurs just as boys are starting to change, just when they are supposed to be going through the transition from boy to young man. It is also exactly the time when in all indigenous communities a boy would have underwent a Rite of Passage (ROP). Now, instead, it is the time when boys are most likely to go off the rails and when they are at greatest risk of the many issues that can threaten their wellbeing and affect them for the rest of their lives.

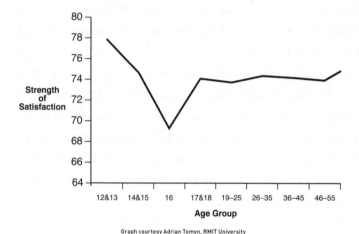

Graph courtesy Adrian Tomyn, RMIT University

As a doctor and a father I do not believe that the nose-dive shown in the graph is a natural part of growing up. I believe that there is something fundamental missing in our culture today that we must relearn – the ability and knowledge of how to support our sons to make a healthy transition from boys to young men. Many loving and motivated parents feel lost and powerless at this time as they watch their boys struggle. It is obvious their sons are having a hard time but any attempts to help just seem to make the situation worse.

A young man's needs

As I have said, a young man is not just a bigger version of a boy. Sure, they are the same person, but they function and think in very different ways and it's important to understand this.

How we parent at this time in their lives and the level to which the community gets involved in creating a healthy transition from boy to young man is critical. It *is* possible to support our boys so that as young men they can be inspired and motivated to really go for it in life. It doesn't mean that it won't still be hard for them at times; it doesn't mean they won't go on the puberty roller coaster; it doesn't mean they won't have struggles and issues. What it *does* mean is that they won't feel alone, they will be able to learn from others' stories, they will know they have gifts and talents which are seen and appreciated, and they will know they are loved and that they have an important role to play both in their community and the wider world.

When we treat our young men simply as big boys they are likely to do one or more of the following:

1. Withdraw and stop communicating
2. Become angry
3. Rebel in any way they can
4. Become depressed.

The missing link

In the early 1990s I went camping for four days with a group of fifty or so men. When we got to the campsite, we were told we were not allowed to talk about sport, politics, what work we did or what car we drove. For the first hour no one really said much at all. Eventually the conversations began and over the course of the four days I was astonished to discover that most of the men were struggling to deal with the same basic issues:

1. Their relationships with their fathers and feeling like they had never been acknowledged by them
2. Not knowing what they were really supposed to be doing with their lives (and knowing that what they were doing wasn't actually it)
3. Wondering when they were going to truly feel like they were a man
4. Trying to work out how to have a healthy relationship with a woman
5. Trying to work out how to best father their own kids.

The revelations and discussions at that camp continued long after we got home. At the time, much of my work involved dealing with men who were struggling with addictions. Those addictions could be alcohol or tobacco but they could also be to work, food, unhealthy relationships, or even exercise. At the core of the addiction was a self-esteem or personal wellbeing issue and almost inevitably these issues began when the men were teenagers. It made so much sense and yet it was demoralising. It was the beginning of the end of my career as a doctor in clinical practice. I wanted to spend my time *preventing* problems – not treating them thirty or forty years later.

I knew that if we could do something for boys as they were becoming young men, we could have a positive influence on their later lives. This period can be a time of great learning where knowledge of the ways of his community and of men is passed on. It certainly is a time when he must stop acting and being treated like a boy. It is a time when his individual gifts and talents must be recognised so that he can begin to take his rightful place within his community. And it is a time when he needs mentors – men other than his father – to guide him and to discipline him.

After twenty years of studying Rites of Passage (ROP) and running programs all over Australia and around the world, I have seen first-hand how when done properly they have a huge impact. Properly-run ROPs help our boys to become confident, capable, balanced and insightful adults with empathy and resilience who are able to handle life's challenges and opportunities.

Before we move on to the specific aspects of good parenting and creating a modern-day Rite of Passage, there is one other crucial aspect of a young man's life we need to get to grips with: technology.

Key Points from Chapter 3

- Boys and young men misbehave and act out when they are not getting their basic needs met

- The needs of a young man are different from those of a boy

- A boy's feeling of wellbeing peaks at age twelve and bottoms out at age sixteen

- Every indigenous society and community created a Rite of Passage (ROP) for their boys when they reached puberty

CHAPTER 4

Gen Zs and the digital age

If your son was born after 1989 then he is part of what's known as Generation Z – or simply Gen Z. He has more opportunities than any other previous generation but his life experiences and way of thinking are also radically different. Here are some points to note about Gen Zs:

- They were born after the World Wide Web was introduced and mobile phones were readily available so they have never known a world without them
- Through their various electronic devices, they are the most *connected* of any generation and spend an average of six hours per day looking at electronic screens
- Many Gen Zs would prefer to learn online via a webinar than in a classroom with a real teacher and other students
- They are unsure about the safety of the world they live in as they have experienced global terrorism like 9/11, they have great concerns about climate change and how it will impact them in their lifetimes, and they are aware of the global financial crisis
- They are the least physically active of any previous

generation – spending hours on their computers instead of playing outdoors
- They are the most highly medicated of any previous generation – it is estimated that in some communities fifteen to twenty per cent of boys are on prescribed psycho-stimulant drugs for behaviour disorders and ten per cent are on anti-depressants.

Gen Zs must deal with all of the typical issues of previous generations, such as depression, drugs and alcohol, risk-taking behaviour, ADHD, gangs, peer pressure and youth suicide. They also face a truly modern-day phenomenon that no generation before has ever experienced: the digital age.

If your son was born into the digital age, he has been constantly exposed to mobile phones, computers and mass communication technology. He is a native to the language of computers and all things technological.

Anyone like me who was born before the beginning of Gen Y (around 1977) is an immigrant in the world of computers. We may speak the lingo quite well, poorly, or not at all, but for most of us it does not come naturally. Gen Zs are not only comfortable with all things digital, many of them can also fix technology when it goes wrong – they intuitively understand what they are doing! It's not that surprising: Gen Zs are literally bathed in the influence of computers from birth. Throughout their childhoods most will have access to multiple computers at home, school, and friends' houses.

Recently, a mate told me that his fifteen-month-old son can swipe his iPhone and find pictures to scroll through. The kid can't even talk or walk but he can use an iPhone!

Smart phones – which in addition to making phone calls are also small mobile computers offering access to social networking and the World Wide Web – are fast becoming a common possession. At the time of writing, over eighty-five per cent of fourteen- to seventeen-year-old boys own a mobile phone and the average age they are obtaining them is fifteen. That age is dropping by two to three years every year. In the next few years all phones will be 'smart' and before long it will be normal for eight-year-olds to own them.

So what do they do with their devices? They use them – all the time. One recent study showed that some teens send or receive an average of 3000 text messages each month and that many are clocking up an average of six to eight hours screen time *per day*. Besides the increased risk of obesity, prompted not only by inactivity but also the disruption of food and hunger cues, excessive screen time reduces the attention span because of its effects on the neurotransmitter dopamine.

Research into sleep patterns of fourteen-year-olds shows that despite needing 8.5 hours per night they are averaging closer to 6.5 due to staying up late social networking, playing games or texting. Even when parents insist that devices are turned off before bedtime, many teenagers spend hours more under the covers on their phones social networking. They contact their friends at any time of the night so that the ping or vibration response constantly interrupts their sleep. Chronic tiredness is a serious side-effect of device overuse. It can affect your son's ability to concentrate at school and impair his moods.

Cyber bullying – the use of the internet and related technologies to psychologically harm other people in a deliberate, repeated and hostile manner – has become a major issue. Targeted attacks can have devastating consequences. Research by the Queensland Government found that more than a quarter of year 4 to year 9 students were bullied every few weeks or more. For some years now, we have been hearing of suicides among teenagers which bear a direct consequence of being bullied online.

Sex and the internet

'Sexting' is a phenomenon where people take sexually explicit photos of themselves and then either text them or post them online. Eighteen per cent of teenage boys say they have posted nude or semi-nude pictures or videos of themselves online.

Sexual conquests are often openly communicated with little regard for the feelings or situation of the other party. At a time when young men are discovering their sexuality and exploring what relationships mean to them, putting it all out in the public arena is highly inappropriate and can have serious and irreversible consequences.

Statistics indicate that almost all fifteen-year-old boys will have viewed pornography online and that many of them watch it regularly. Boys as young as eight are now accessing porn and it is estimated that porn accounts for over thirty per cent of all internet traffic. Many boys grow up thinking that what they are seeing is normal and acceptable behaviour. Much of the porn is degrading to women who are portrayed as objects available for the pleasure of men, regardless of what that may involve. This is where our sons are learning about sex (and the young girls who are also watching it think that's the way it's supposed to be).

> Eighteen-year-old Kirsty talks about her boyfriend Thai. 'He watches porn every day. For him it's just normal. He lets me watch it with him sometimes but he never wants to talk about it. He gets really angry if I mention it. He also masturbates watching porn a lot. And then he wants me to do what the girls in the pictures are doing. I'm not a porn star – I'm his girlfriend. Sometimes I think he prefers porn because our sex life isn't that great. Most of my girlfriends tell me their boyfriends also watch porn. It's a bit sick I reckon but I don't feel like there is anything I can do about it.'

Most parents have little or no idea how to control their kids' addiction to technology. This is understandable as it is a first generation issue and most parents have little or no prior experience dealing with it. To complicate matters, the kids are usually better at using computers than their parents and can easily hide what they are getting up to. McAfee, the world's largest technology security company, released findings from their '2012 Teen Internet Behavior' study. The study investigated the online habits, behaviours, interests and lifestyles of the first generation to truly grow up online. It revealed how teens are not only engaging in risky behaviours, but how they are hiding it from their parents, many of whom don't realise they are being fooled. Seventy per cent of teenagers say they hide things they do online from their parents with the most common way of doing so being that they clear the internet history browser after they finish using the computer.

Reality distortion and the internet

There is a reality distortion issue with the internet and many young people are literally getting lost in cyberspace. I remember watching two boys playing a soccer game on the computer. They were able to choose their players from all the best leagues in the world and the positions for them to play in. They knew so much about it, were having so much fun, and it was a great battle. However, at first I couldn't understand when at the end they wanted to check who was best on the field and to watch highlights of particular moments. I realised with horror that on some level they felt the game they had just played was real.

This reality distortion is everywhere. Social networking leads kids to believe that all their online friends are real and important, often more important than their families and real friends, even though they may have never even met them.

The digital divide

The 'digital divide' describes the different ways in which teenagers relate to and deal with technology. There are those kids for whom the digital world has become a way to spend *all* their social time. I call them the 'techno slaves'. They spend (or should I say, waste) hours and hours watching the screen and playing games. They will play the same game repetitively – on desktop computers, on portable gaming consoles or on their smart phones. They surf the web randomly and look for things to do which have little or no purpose. They flick between Facebook, Twitter, YouTube, email, texts and Instagram or whatever happens to be the latest fad. Social networking sites become their identity and they spend vast amounts of time sending messages to their hundreds or even thousands of friends – most of whom they most likely have never met.

Then there is another group of teenagers who actually *engage* with technology. I call them the 'techno creators'. They make music or their own video clips, they write code, they create apps, they innovate. Techno creators use social networking as a way to communicate with friends so that they can meet up as well as being able to keep track of what is going on with each other. Importantly, techno creators also have active and engaged lives *outside* of the digital world. They know what they want to do and technology helps them achieve it.

Dealing with technology

You cannot win the battle against technology by simply using parental locks or internet filters. Restricting your son's online access won't work either. You may be successful for a period while he's a boy but inevitably he will just go underground and you won't have a clue what he's up to.

Whether your son is a techno slave or a techno creator, as a parent you *must* get involved and become aware. Your son needs your understanding, your input and your support. No generation before has ever had so much technological influence and your son is unlikely to be able to effectively navigate it all by himself.

As his parent or carer, you need to understand as much as you possibly can about the digital world that he inhabits, starting from when he first engages with computers and gaming. Get him to teach you, to show you what he does and to explain how it all works to you. It may take some time and effort, but you will be amazed at what you discover.

You will have input and be able to discuss with him what usage is appropriate and how much of his time and energy should be spent on digital pursuits. This gives you the ability to negotiate and set mutually agreed upon boundaries. Left to his own devices, your son is likely to over-indulge. If you try and set all the rules then he will simply seek to do it anyway without your knowing.

Your son needs your ongoing support as new technology enters his world. At some stage, he will confront cyber bullying; strangers may befriend him and want to meet up; he may have photos of himself 'tagged' by others and made public without his approval and he will certainly be exposed to pornography. He needs to be able to talk to you about all of these issues so that he knows he has your support and does not have to work it all out by himself.

Ultimately, it will be his decision as to what sort of relationship he has with technology. We need to accept as parents or carers that while we can no longer tell him what to do, there is a lot that we *can* do to help him make wise decisions. That's what the next part of this book is all about.

Key Points from Chapter 4

- Technology is having a major impact on the lives of boys and young men

- The 'digital divide' separates those who simply waste time with technology and those who use it as a valuable tool

- Cyber bullying, internet pornography and reality distortion are all part of your sons' lives

- You need to understand and get involved with technology

PART 2

GETTING OUR BOYS READY FOR THE WORLD

CHAPTER 5

You can't start raising a teenager once he actually becomes a teenager

Stephen is forty-four. 'I remember as a kid my dad always seemed to be at work. He left early in the morning and often wasn't home until after I was in bed. On weekends he spent lots of time in his office, except for Saturday afternoon when he played golf with his mates. He really had very little to do with me. I don't think he ever came and watched me play sport or came to my school plays.

'When I was about fifteen I got into trouble at school. A group of us took the day off and went to the beach. We got caught and because it was a private school where you weren't supposed to do that sort of thing there was quite a fuss about it and the headmaster rang my parents. My dad came home early and he called me into his office and then started to give me a lecture. He was sitting at his desk telling me all about how important it was to do well at school if I wanted to get a good job later on. He talked about how hard he had worked and he just went on and on. I stood there and I remember how angry I was. Who was this person to all of a sudden be telling me how to live my life when he actually knew almost nothing about me? The truth is that I'd been feeling angry with my dad for quite some time but that was the day it all came to a head. It ended up in a shouting match and then my dad told me that I was grounded for something ridiculous like six months. It never happened because I just went out anyway and he wasn't even around to do anything about it and my mum didn't want to get involved. I lost a lot of respect for my dad after that.'

This is a mistake that is unfortunately made by many fathers who think that, despite not having been particularly involved or present in their son's life, they can just step in when their boy starts acting out and tell him what to do. By this stage it is too late and he is not going to want to listen to you telling him how to live his life.

There are two important things we need to be aware of with our boys when they are young:

1. They are watching us and they will copy what we do now and later in life.
2. How we parent them at a younger age will make a huge difference in our ability to stay connected to them once they become teenagers.

Patrick is forty-one and runs a software business. 'My mother was amazing when I was growing up. One of her favourite sayings was, "Family is the most important thing. When you're dying you won't be wishing you'd spent more time at work." We had dinner together as a family nearly every night and we all used to take turns to talk about what we'd done during the day. She loved watching me play sport and she got on really well with my friends. They all thought she was great.

'Now as a father myself, I can see how much her attitudes have influenced me. I always make sure that I am home in time for dinner and we do lots together as a family. Mum is still a very important part of our family and my children adore spending time with their Nana. I've learned so much from her and I often ask myself the question when I don't know what to do, "What would Mum do?"'

Thirty-five-year-old Elliot works as a motor mechanic. 'My father always used to say, "Do as I say and not as I do". I really bloody hated that and it didn't seem fair or right. He also used to say, "I make the rules but I don't have to keep them". We fought a lot when I was growing up. I hated that he did things like hitting me over the back of the head if I spoke to Mum badly and telling me I had to be respectful. Then he would turn around and swear at her five minutes later for the stupidest thing like his steak being overcooked. The worst of it is that now I find myself doing that with my kids. The other day after work I was telling my son how important it was to live healthy and I was smoking a cigarette and drinking a can of cola. I'm also pretty overweight now and I could just see the way he was looking at me. I saw myself in his eyes looking at my dad and I didn't like it at all.'

Have you ever found yourself doing something only to realise, maybe even with horror, that you are becoming your father or your mother? Our actions and attitudes influence those of our children – they are watching us all the time. During their first years they will literally mimic everything we do – good or bad.

Back when I was nine or ten a lot of adults smoked. After one of my parents' dinner parties I stole some of the cigarettes they had put out for the guests. My sister and I used to take our dog for a walk each day. The next day instead of going on our usual walk we went and hid in some bushes and smoked cigarettes. Actually, we tried to smoke cigarettes but they made us cough too much, so we just held them and pretended to be 'adults'.

Children of parents who smoke are more likely themselves to smoke; the same thing applies to children whose parents drink. In fact, all behaviours and attitudes that parents exhibit – good and bad – influence their children. If parents are involved in community work or have a passion for travelling then there is an increased chance their children will be the same.

I remember as a twelve-year-old going skiing with my father. He was a real adventurer and sometimes we would be out in blizzard conditions with almost no one else on the mountain. It would be cold and challenging but he seemed to enjoy it more the worse it got. I would happily tag along because it was so special to have my father all to myself. To this day when I surf or go bushwalking if ever the weather turns and it becomes windy, cold and wet, I get this feeling of joy and excitement that overcomes me. I think about being up on the mountain with my dad.

The way my father brought me up was influenced by the way his father brought him up and so on back through the generations. Same with my mother. Knowing this creates quite a responsibility. What we as parents or carers do and how we are will not only influence our children but will have an effect on their children and their children's children, and beyond. If we want our kids to be a certain way then the best thing for us to do is to be that way ourselves. Children learn most not by what we say but what we *do*.

When he's young, your son will want to be as close as possible to you. Hanging out with his dad (or mum) will be his favourite pastime, except maybe for watching TV or playing computer games. The important thing for a young boy is that he feels loved and has as strong a connection as possible with his parents. He wants to be held, to be cuddled, to play together and to be told a hundred times a day that he is loved and wonderful. He thinks you know everything, you can solve all the problems and that you will be there forever.

How to parent young boys

Over the years, there have been many different theories as to how we should bring up our kids. In the Victorian era it was believed that children should be seen and not heard. At dinner time these boys and girls were dressed in their finest clothes and expected to sit at the table in silence. In the post-war period, discipline was considered highly important and there was even a saying, 'Spare the rod and spoil the child'. Many youngsters suffered regular beatings which were considered an appropriate and even necessary way to help them learn life's fundamental lessons.

As a result of the hippy revolution in the 1960s and 70s, there were children whose parents felt that they should have no boundaries and be able to do whatever they liked in order for their creativity be allowed to fully flourish. These children were often seen late at night at parties having conversations with adults who were high on drugs and who thought these kids were amazing and had such wisdom even though they were only eight years old. Unfortunately, many of these same children started smoking marijuana and experimenting with drugs before they were even teenagers and their parents' attempts to try and control them failed as they had never learned the concept of appropriate boundaries.

I have looked at a lot of research and developed a set of key skills or developmental strategies that you can use during your son's formative years. At this time of their lives, boys will be open to our influence and good parenting makes a big difference. Here are seven things you can do that will be highly beneficial:

1. **Spend regular one-on-one time together**, preferably with your mobile phone and other devices switched off. Your son will love this more than anything. Mums tend to do this naturally but for dads it varies. Some fathers do while others are always in their own world. Even when they are around they are on the phone, reading the newspaper, watching television or just not *present*. You can't spend all your spare time with your son but you can make times when he really knows it is just you and him. Try and find things that you both love doing. It may be going out for breakfast or hot chocolate on a Sunday morning, kicking a ball after school, playing a game of chess or building a model aeroplane together – the possibilities are endless. It's a great way to grow your relationship, increase emotional attachment and build his sense of security.

2. **Make a habit of acknowledging your son's qualities and encouraging him to pursue his individual gifts and talents.** I have mentioned this already and I will do so again because it is so important and fundamental to the wellbeing of your son. Not all boys do well at all things, however they all have some great qualities and it is important

they are not just judged on their achievements. They need to know what their qualities are and they need to hear it from you. If your son does something kind then acknowledge him for it. If he is compassionate and caring then let him know that you see it and that you believe it is a great quality. If there is something that he loves doing, whether or not it is something that you have talent in, like music, art, building things, surfing or gardening, then encourage and support him in that area. Who knows, it may be what he ends up doing with his life or it may become a lifelong hobby that gives him enormous satisfaction. Plus, if he has active interests then he is much less likely to fill in all his spare time staring at a computer screen.

3. **Share stories with your son about what you did when you were his age.** This is a perfect way for him to learn about you and it will have such a positive effect on your relationship. Boys want to know what life was like for you. I used to love listening to the stories my parents told me when we were in the car going away on holidays. I was fascinated by how different life was when they were young before television and computers. My boys were the same and enjoyed it when I told them my stories, especially the ones where I had adventures or got into trouble. It is also important to make a habit of really listening to *his* stories and what is going

on for him. This will complete the 'storytelling circle' and will allow you to maintain an ongoing and open relationship. The aim is to continue this sharing of stories into his teenage years so that he can know what it was like for you at that time, and what you struggled with, and also for your son to share what is going on for him at a time when it is so vital to have open, trusting communication.

4. **Teach your son how to reflect on things.** This will enable him to critically assess situations and learn wise decision-making – despite what other people may be saying or doing. Use life experiences, movies, books and so forth to ask reflective questions. For example, if you see someone smoking don't tell your son not to smoke when he is older because it is unhealthy. Instead, ask him what he thinks about people smoking and whether he is going to smoke when he is older. Or if in a film you watch someone teasing or bullying another person, ask your son what he thinks about that sort of behaviour. You may well be surprised and impressed by the answers you get. It also allows him to ask questions and can lead to some wonderful and important conversations. I am constantly amazed by the wisdom and insight of young boys when they are given a chance to express their thoughts.

5. **Help your son solve his own problems.** This will stimulate brain development and increase life skills. Rather than you doing everything for him, support him as he grows older to devise solutions himself. Teach him to identify options so he can make choices for solving problems and then let him have a go. It may be something small like how to organise his toys in his room, or it may be something bigger like how to deal with a younger sibling who annoys him or kids at school who tease him. Have the discussion and see if you can come up with a solution together with as much input as possible from him. Failing or succeeding is not what it's about, rather it's the process of thinking it through, having a go and then seeing the result that is important.

6. **Start the process of connecting privileges with responsibility.** It is crucial that by the time your son is a teenager he understands this link so he can learn personal responsibility. He needs to learn that he is not just going to get things without being responsible and that if he is irresponsible then those things may actually be taken away. Pocket money is a great example and should be tied into doing certain jobs around the house or behaving in an appropriate manner. As an adult, it's unlikely he will be paid for work he does not do or that he will be able to be rude or abusive to his colleagues

or boss without being fired. Much better that he learns this when he is young and still at home. I will talk about this again later as one of the key skills a teenager must have and one which all too often they have not learned as youngsters.

7. **When your son misbehaves and discipline is required, separate the person from the behaviour.** We need to be able to tell our sons when their behaviour is not okay and we need to be able to do it in a way that they get the message and learn but are not shamed or wounded. Physical violence like beatings or using a belt are absolutely not okay no matter what he has done. The aim is to be gentle on the person and firm on the behaviour, so he knows that you still love him even though you are not happy about what has happened. Never shame him or tell him that he is useless and unworthy. The goal here is to teach your son that while certain behaviours are unacceptable, he is always loved and he needs to learn from the experience. An example may be if your son takes money from your wallet and buys sweets. (I remember doing that, sorry Mum!) You might choose to tell him what a bad person he is, how he is a little thief and if he keeps doing it he will end up in jail when he is older, then you might smack him and send him to bed with no dinner. Alternatively, you could tell him that you love him, that you know he is a really

trustworthy boy and that you are sad that he has stolen from you. You could ask him gently why he did it, for which he may or may not have an answer. You could then ask him if he thinks stealing is okay and whether it is something that he wants to keep doing. If consequences are required, you should be able to explain why to him rather than punishing him from a place of anger. You could then explain that when people steal they usually get punished and see if together you can agree what would be a fair outcome. For example, no pocket money that week, or not being allowed to play on the computer for a few days. I suggest that you then once again tell him that even though he has stolen from you and that such behaviour is not okay, you love him and give him a big hug.

Obviously, you have to use your commonsense in these situations, but if you can practise separating the person from the behaviour, as your son grows older and really starts to push the boundaries, you will be able to maintain your healthy relationship with him.

Critically, if the misbehaving is actually a cry for help or if he happens to find himself in really serious trouble, it is vital that he knows he can come to you. While you may not support his behaviour, he needs to know you will not reject him and that he can to turn to you for help and advice.

The whole situation is going to change

As our boys grow up, no matter how sweet and loving they have been, no matter how involved we have been as parents, there is a good chance that at some stage they will become non-communicative, disrespectful, rude, and disagree with practically everything we have to say. This is when the home can turn into a war zone and the teenage years can result in a breakdown in family relations that can stretch well into adult life.

It doesn't have to be a disaster though. How your son deals with everything that is happening will depend very much upon how he feels about himself, and whether or not he has what I call a healthy 'Personal Identity'.

There are also natural shifts in a boy's relationship with both dad and mum that *must happen* as he becomes a young man. As I have said, how you parent a young man needs to be *totally* different from how you parent a boy. If we can support and honour these shifts, rather than ignoring or actively resisting them, then we can maintain healthy relations with our sons into adult life. If we try to deny these changes, then we risk losing our loving connection – which we might never get back.

In the next three chapters, we will look at what influences your son's Personal Identity, and the critical and specific changes that have to happen in the relationships between fathers and sons, and mothers and sons.

Key Points from Chapter 5

- Be involved as much as you can in your son's life when he is still a boy

- Good parenting involves spending one-on-one time with your kids, sharing stories and teaching the skills of resilience and problem solving

- When discipline is required, always separate the person from the behaviour

CHAPTER 6

How to give our sons what they need

Jonah is sixteen. He wants to be an engineer. He doesn't find school easy but he tries hard because he knows that's what he has to do to get the marks he needs to go to university. He works at the local newsagency on Saturdays and is saving up for an electric guitar. He loves music and he and his mates have started a band. Jonah is now a bit taller than his dad and can run faster than him. They wrestle a lot and he is amazed to find that sometimes he can hold his dad down. Jonah gets on well with his dad's mates, especially a guy called Pete who is a surfer and taught him how to catch waves last summer. They talked for hours about Pete's adventures travelling and surfing all over the world.

Jonah loves his mum and is really close to her even though sometimes he feels she is a bit over-protective. What he loves best is when they sit in the kitchen while she is cooking and just chat about what they have both been doing. Jonah has a group of friends he has known since he was young and they have lots of fun together. Some of the kids at school are doing drugs but Jonah and his mates think they are losers. He would love a girlfriend and recently has started walking home from school with Charlotte who he has a crush on but he feels really shy.

Otis is fifteen. He hates school. He thinks it's a waste of time and often doesn't go or leaves halfway through the day. He has no idea what he wants to do when he finishes school and says he doesn't care. Otis's dad has a real estate business, works hard and is often home late and out on weekends. When he is home they either don't talk or they fight. Otis feels his dad is always putting him down and nothing he ever does is good enough. His dad is always trying to tell him what to do and says that unless Otis starts studying and getting serious about life, like he was at his age, then he will never amount to anything.

Otis spends lots of time in his room playing games on his computer. Often he plays until 1 or 2 in the morning. It makes it hard to get up and then he sometimes falls asleep in class. He doesn't have many friends but recently he started hanging out with a couple of guys who came to his school after being expelled from another school. They go into the city on the weekends and find a way to buy alcohol which they drink as quickly as they can. Sometimes they have competitions to see who can steal things from people's front gardens. Last weekend Otis stole a statue and got chased down the street by the owner of the house.

One of the guys introduced Otis to marijuana. At first he hated the way it made him feel but he kept doing it because the others were. Now he really enjoys being stoned and they have started meeting up before school to have a smoke.

What sort of a teenager will your son be?

Even if a young boy is healthy and happy, this does not tell us how he is going to be as a young man. Research has shown that up to the age of twelve, boys are the happiest they will ever be. Then, between fourteen and eighteen, their wellbeing plummets to its lowest level.

So, what makes the difference to how our sons deal with the crucial teenage years? What can we do to support them to be happy and motivated while avoiding the minefield of negative influences?

We first need to examine what sort of men we want them to be. A really good place to aim for is one where are sons:

1. Make healthy and wise decisions
2. Are passionate about their lives and what they do
3. Have a personal set of respectful values to live by
4. Know they are loved and are an important part of a community
5. Are resilient and able to overcome challenges that inevitably will arise.

We then need to ask ourselves what exactly we can do to help. We also need to know what we should *not* do. Once our sons are teenagers we can't live their lives for them, we can't rescue them (even if we want to), we can't tell them what to do or how to be, we can't even expect to know everything they get up to. What we *can* do is support them by setting the right example, giving them key life skills, identifying and acknowledging their individual gifts and talents, helping them find their own values, and loving them for who they are.

A healthy Personal Identity is the key

In order for your son to become a happy and successful young man, it is critical that he develops a healthy Personal Identity. Armed with a healthy Personal Identity he will have a strong sense of self, good values and a feeling of belonging. This will bring out the best in him and you will see the caring, courageous, fun-loving, kind, romantic, strong, loyal young man who will be inspired to do something meaningful with his life. He will also have the skills to successfully navigate his way through his world and avoid many of the pitfalls.

If your son doesn't develop a healthy Personal Identity, he will likely be unsure of his beliefs and will feel insecure and confused about himself and the future. This will impact on everything he does. He may become angry, withdrawn, depressed, non-communicative, unmotivated and negative. He'll be at a greater risk of becoming addicted to digital devices, drugs, alcohol or inappropriate risky behaviours. His chances of suffering from depression will also greatly increase.

A healthy Personal Identity is the key to a young man doing well and avoiding ending up places he doesn't want to be. Possessing a healthy Personal Identity can combat so many of the issues facing young men today. I have seen first-hand how some young men, like Jonah, are into just about everything on offer. They love their sport, they play musical instruments and have hobbies. They're fun to be around, and they have a good group of friends. When you ask them what they want to do when they leave school they may not know exactly, but they will be very clear that they want to do *something*.

I have also met many young men, like Otis, who think that life sucks and everything is working against them. They are angry, spend hours playing violent computer games, wear caps or hoodies all the time and don't want to talk. When I ask them what they want to do when they leave school the answer is all too often, 'Don't know and don't care.'

It is not hard to see that a young man like Jonah who has a healthy Personal Identity will be far less likely to get into drugs or join a gang. I remember asking one eighteen-year-old whether he was into drugs. His reply was, 'No way, I've worked too hard to stuff up my head with drugs. There's too much that I want to do!'

Otis is at much greater risk. Drugs or hanging out with kids who are a bad influence will make him feel good for a while. If his friends are doing it then he probably will too. Otis doesn't perceive much hope for what life has to offer so he is less likely to think about the consequences of his actions.

The Personal Identity (PI) scale

There are five key factors which contribute to a young man's healthy Personal Identity and I have developed a scale which allows us to measure them.

The five factors are:

1. Healthy family relationships
2. Key life skills
3. Good physical health
4. Recognition of and encouragement to pursue his unique gifts and talents
5. Support through the transition from boy to young man.

The chart below will allow you to assess the Personal Identity wellbeing of your boy. As you read it you should be able to easily identify which category for each of the factors he fits into. A score of 2, 1 or 0 is given for each factor giving a maximum score of 10.

	Score 2	Score 1	Score 0
Healthy family relationships	Enjoys spending time with his mum and dad but also has his own life and friends. Talks freely about what is going on for him and is comfortable to ask for advice or help when needed. Feels trusted by his parents and there is no need for them to know what he is doing every moment. Knows that he can come to them if he has a problem and talk about it.	May feel tense when he is with his mum or dad and communicates a lot less. Still has times when they enjoy doing things together but it is becoming less common. Arguments happen but can usually be resolved. Parents are aware that he has a private life and are very concerned about what he gets up to but he often doesn't tell them. May or may not talk to his parents if he is in trouble or worried about something.	Almost zero communication happening and/or lot of arguments. Seems angry or shut down when he is around his mum or dad who have very little idea what is going on in his life. Doesn't talk to parents or carers about what is going on and if he has problems they would be the last people he would talk to.

	Score 2	Score 1	Score 0
Key life skills	Able to talk and communicate his feelings well. Gets on with people of all ages. Can be trusted that if he agrees to do something that he will do it. If he makes a mistake he can learn from it and is happy to seek advice from older people. Thinks about the impact on others when he does things. Has lots of creative ideas when there is a problem and enjoys working with other people.	Communicates sometimes and at others is shut down. Has friends but mainly his own age and may struggle to make new ones. Sometimes does what he says and at others won't. If he makes a mistake he may have another go but sometimes gives up. Rarely asks for advice. At times seems very aware of those around him and at others quite selfish. Sometimes gets creative ideas but needs to be pushed and often prefers to do things alone.	Very poor communicator and has very few friends. Can't be trusted to do what he says. If he makes a mistake he gives up, blames something or someone and sees himself as useless and hopeless. Never asks for or listens to advice. Appears very selfish and to only think of himself. Won't look for creative solutions to problems and could definitely be described as a loner.

	Score 2	Score 1	Score 0
Good physical health	Exercises regularly alone, with friends or through sport. Is healthy and rarely gets sick. Only eats junk food occasionally. Is not overweight. Sleeps well and has plenty of energy.	Exercises sporadically. Gets sick a few times a year. Eats quite a bit of junk food. Could be healthier and may be a bit overweight. Likes to stay up late and sleep in when he can.	Rarely if ever exercises. Is often sick. Eats lots of junk food. May be overweight or very skinny. Stays up really late, will stay in bed until lunchtime if allowed to and always seems tired.
Recognition of and encouragement to pursue his unique gifts and talents	Has hobbies, is passionate and motivated about what he does, knows what he is good at and practises hard to get better. Parents and school friends support him to do what he loves. Uses technology to keep in touch with friends and assist him with his activities.	Has things he is good at but doesn't often do them even though he really enjoys them when he does. Tends to jump from one thing to another a lot. Is quite influenced by what everyone else is doing. Can tend to waste time with technology playing computer games and social networking.	Doesn't know what he wants to do. Feels like he is hopeless and isn't good at anything. Doesn't really have any hobbies. Spends a significant amount of time watching TV or on his computer.

	Score 2	Score 1	Score 0
Support through the transition from boy to young man	Took part in an event that acknowledged he is now a young man. His parents give him greater privileges and he can take on responsibilities and look after himself. Has older men including his father and mentors who he talks to.	Slips between acting like a boy and a young man and his parents sometimes still treat him like a child. Is not yet independent and at times is responsible and at others not. Sometimes talks to his father or older men but not often.	No acknowledge-ment that he is becoming a young man and still acts like a child especially with his parents. Struggles to look after himself even on a basic level. Doesn't talk to or seek advice from his father, older men or mentors.

Think about your son or a young man that you know and for each of the five factors give him 2, 1 or 0 points to arrive at his PI score. This will tell you a lot about how he is going in his life and the current state of his wellbeing. It will also determine how he feels about himself. It will be the very foundation upon which he makes his decisions and builds his life now and into the future.

Going well: a score of 8–10 on the PI scale

A score of between 8 and 10 indicates that a young man is in a good situation and will be likely to:

- Know he has the ability to make decisions that influence his direction in life
- See himself as being capable of setting goals and successfully completing them
- Feel that he has the support and love of his family and the people around him
- Be able to fail when he tries something and see that as a learning experience rather than as a sign that he is useless.

This young man knows he has the ability to create a meaningful life, and feels like he has some level of control and influence over his path. He sees options and possibilities, senses that he has potential and that he can move out of a current situation and into a better one. He will feel confident to look for a part-time job, to save up for a car or a holiday, decide to learn a trade or do a course to improve his employment opportunities. He will be motivated to finish school and go on to tertiary education and if not, there will be something else that he wants to do. He is likely to play sport or have other hobbies.

If a young man scores 0 for one of the factors but is high in the others he can still do well. For example, if a young man has health issues but a loving family situation, has basic life skills, is aware of what he is good at and feels supported, then he will be much more able to approach life with a positive attitude. I knew a young man who was wheelchair-bound after a car accident and who had all sorts of associated health problems, including sores on his buttocks and recurrent infections from a permanent catheter. However, his family adored him and were very close-knit. He was a great communicator, had incredible resilience, loved his music and sang in a band, plus was given lots of support through his teenage years by older men, especially his grandfather and an uncle. He was one of the happiest and most popular kids I have ever met and we were all amazed by his love of life despite his obvious hardships.

Could go either way: a score of 5–7 on the PI scale

In my experience, the majority of young men today fall within this category. We know they are great kids because we have watched them grow up but we can also see that they are struggling, awkward and often their communication is poor. A score of between 5 and 7 indicates a young man is at risk and needs some help. If he gets the right support he will do really well but we also need to be aware that this young man is vulnerable to people and things that could lead him down a path that may not be in his best interests.

This young man may:

- Lack confidence in his ability to make decisions that influence his life, but with support will be able to improve this skill
- Have difficulty setting goals and successfully completing them and may well need extra help to do so
- Place very high value on getting support and acknowledgement from his peers which may be conditional upon him doing what they want
- Consider giving up if he fails when he tries something and really needs someone to tell him that it is okay and does not mean that he is useless.

Critically at risk: a score of 0–4 on the PI scale

One way to demonstrate the importance of a high wellbeing score on the PI scale is to examine the impact of a score between 0 and 4. I have worked with young men who are in juvenile justice detention centres for crimes ranging from theft to aggravated assault. When I ask them about their lives and score them on the PI scale what they reveal is often totally tragic. It is not uncommon that they've had abusive situations at home, they have very poor basic life skills, they don't like themselves, have little or no support from adults, and generally hate the world.

Young men with a PI score of 0–4 usually:

- Don't get on with their families
- Have low self-esteem
- Struggle to communicate their feelings and deal with conflict
- Eat lots of junk food and don't exercise. Smoke or do drugs (or engage in other unhealthy activities)
- Even though they are in a man's body still feel and are treated like a boy.

This young man believes he is powerless and his life is out of control. He may well feel that he is useless, unable to achieve anything and that nobody really cares about him. He is likely to become withdrawn and internalise his feelings or act out inappropriately. He's also at much greater risk of becoming depressed, getting involved with the wrong sort of peer group and getting into trouble, which of course will only reinforce his negative feelings.

How to combat the influence of technology, drugs, alcohol and peer group pressure

A young man's PI score directly affects how he'll get on in life. As parents or carers we cannot keep him in cotton-wool forever. When he's young, we can control his exposure to the internet, what he watches on TV, what food he eats, and his choice of friends. By the time he's a teenager your son is making his own decisions whether you like it or not, and these will all be affected by how he sees himself, and whether or not he has a healthy Personal Identity.

This aim of this book is not to focus on the potential problems. While we have to be aware of them, I want to explain what you can do and how we can equip our sons with the necessary wisdom, support and skills to be able to deal with problems when they arise. As you read the case studies, look for the PI factors and see how they impact both positively and negatively. You may even relate to some instances that have been present in your own life.

Samuel is thirty-six and an electrician. 'Gosh it was so weird when I went through puberty. All of a sudden I felt really lost and unsure of myself. I hated having pimples and that all my clothes didn't fit properly. I really felt like I didn't fit in at all. What I loved doing was climbing things. Ever since I was little I'd always climbed everything I could, the trees in the backyard were my speciality. There was a climbing wall on the other side of town but it was really hard to get to by public transport. My dad used to take me there every Saturday afternoon. He would drop me off and go sit in a café and work on his computer. I met a good group of kids there and they became my friends. I actually met my first ever girlfriend there. Later some of us went into climbing competitions together when we got really good at it.

'After we'd finished climbing, Dad would pick me up and drive me home. Sometimes we talked in the car and sometimes we just listened to music together. Often we would get fish and chips on the way home and hang out eating them in the park. Looking back I can see that was a great thing my dad did. I think that getting into climbing and meeting those friends was what kept me from getting into all sorts of trouble when I was a teenager.'

Harry was a patient of mine for many years. His father was a doctor and his mother had a clothing shop. Harry says that he was brought up by babysitters and nannies. As a boy he had a television in his room, could watch whatever he wanted and often stayed up late. They lived in a big house and he had all the latest toys and gadgets. If he needed money he just took it from his mother's purse or his father's wallet. Harry's parents were never there when he got home from school and they rarely ate dinner together. His dad never spent time with him or watched him play sport; he was always too busy.

At fourteen Harry smoked marijuana for the first time. By fifteen he was smoking in his room every night and before school. At seventeen he left school and got into harder drugs and ended up using heroin. Harry stole money from his parents and then started selling items from the family home to support his habit. His parents paid for multiple expensive stints in rehab which worked for a while but he always relapsed. I met Harry when he was twenty-one. He hadn't spoken to his mum or dad for over two years, he was on a methadone program and living in a halfway house in the city.

The number and type of hard drugs readily available is greater than ever. Amphetamines have been refined and purified so that whereas ecstasy was responsible for many problems in the past, ice (which is a pure form) is so addictive that a single dose can leave a person with a habit. When I worked as a doctor in emergency departments I regularly saw young men who were violent and psychotic after taking amphetamines.

Marijuana which used to be grown in people's back-yards is now hydroponically produced and increasingly stronger strains are being developed. The levels of marijuana's active ingredient tetrahydrocannabinol (THC) are much greater in these new strains and can have devastating effects on developing brains. Psychiatric wards all over the country are admitting increasing numbers of young men who after periods of heavy marijuana use have become psychotic and developed schizophrenic symptoms which often require lifelong medication.

These and other drugs are now a part of mainstream culture. They are reasonably accessible and affordable. For the price of a few beers anyone can buy a tablet. Often drugs are supplied free to first-time users. I have seen boys as young as eleven starting to experiment. It is also not uncommon in some schools for some thirteen- to fourteen-year-old boys to be regularly taking drugs on the weekend and then to have that habit increase over time.

We have to accept that our sons will have multiple opportunities to try drugs. These opportunities and exposures to drug-taking cultures only increase as they get older.

The question we need to ask ourselves is not how we are going to keep our sons away from drugs, but what can we do so that when they're offered them, they have the strength and wisdom to say no.

Alcohol is as accessible as ever. Most teenagers can get access to alcohol if they really want to, many parents actually have unlocked cupboards or fridges full of the stuff. Once again, we need to ask ourselves why some kids will get drunk at every opportunity and then get involved in stupid and dangerous behaviour, while others have lots of fun without needing to drink.

Experimentation is normal

The chances are, like us, that our sons will experiment. Think about your own teenage years. Did you ever get drunk, try drugs or do something dangerous or regrettable as a result of peer group pressure? It's normal for young men to experiment – it's a natural part of growing up to do things that are outside the boundaries of so called 'acceptable behaviour'. There is no point pretending it doesn't or won't happen to our sons. While we don't have to agree with it, we need to be there for them at this time.

Young men with a healthy Personal Identity are still likely to experiment, but hopefully they will be older when they do so, and will engage with some level of self-awareness and control. They are less likely to become addicted. They will enjoy many things in life that give them more satisfaction than being drunk or stoned.

Having a low sense of wellbeing is uncomfortable and can make a young person feel as though the world is a difficult and lonely place. Many young men report that for a short time, drugs and alcohol help them feel the way they want to feel – powerful, in control, confident – all the things a young man with a poor Personal Identity doesn't usually feel. The drug then becomes more than just an experiment and turns into a readily available 'fix' for what is missing in his life.

A recovering drug addict once told me that his problems started when his sense of wellbeing and Personal Identity became tied up with being stoned. The only time he felt any good was when he was using drugs, so it didn't take long for him to be wanting to do that all the time.

Steve is a thirty-five-year-old with a long-term drug addiction. 'I first started using when I was fifteen. Some guys I knew were doing it at parties. At first I really didn't want to but they put pressure on me and gave me a hard time when I said no. I have always been shy and found it difficult talking to people I didn't know very well. I certainly wasn't popular and felt lonely a lot of the time. When I got stoned I lost a lot of my inhibitions and all of a sudden I found that I could talk to anybody and have a really good time. It was great to feel popular.

'After that, I always got stoned every time I went to a party. We used to have so much fun. Then I started doing it on my own because I liked the way that it made me feel. It was as if I didn't have problems any more and everything was okay. I started using more and more often. It got out of control.'

Combatting depression by bringing out the best in our young men

I am particularly interested in the causes of and solutions to depression. It worries me enormously both on a personal and a professional level it has become so endemic in young men today. I believe we as a society are creating much of this depression through the pressure young men are feeling to have to be a certain way if they want to be accepted and loved.

In many cases, I believe depression is 'a sickness of the soul' and therefore avoidable. Put simply, if someone is doing what they love then they are much less likely to be depressed. If, on the other hand, they are doing what they do because they are trying to impress or keep someone else happy – but it is not actually *their* truth – then they are at greater risk of succumbing to persistent unhappiness.

The age at which depression is striking is getting younger and the number of young men being afflicted is increasing. Too often the main method of treatment is medication but this can result in side-effects so that instead of ending up with young men who feel depressed we end up with young men who are numb and don't feel anything.

As a father of two I can't think of anything scarier than to see my sons depressed. To see them feeling hopeless about life and needing medication to get through the day. And to fear that the ultimate expression of their condition could result in them taking their own lives and becoming another tragic statistic of youth suicide, which for teenage boys is now the number one cause of death. How can it be that at a certain age our young men start to feel that life is so hopeless that they need medication, or that worse still they decide it is not worth living any more?

My grandfather became depressed after serving in World War II and killed himself. I never got to meet this man who my mother has always spoken about with such admiration and affection. My concern has always been that as an adult, like other members of my family, I would follow suit. I certainly know that my own personality type is one where generally I am happy and energetic but at other times I can feel quite flat.

The medical world recognises two distinct types of depression. The first assumes that within the brain there is a chemical imbalance. This form of internal depression is believed to best be treated with medication to alter the balance of chemicals.

The second form of depression is instigated by outside events. For example, if a family member dies then there is a clear external cause for the depression and with time it should pass. In this external depression, the person feels powerless to change their circumstances and it is only when they can accept what has happened that they can move on.

As a doctor I agree with this medical theory and that there are two forms of depression. What I don't agree with is the statistics around how many cases of depression are internal and how many are external.

Huge numbers of people across the country are being treated for depression with nothing other than medication. Countless numbers of young men in schools, universities and workplaces – nearly ten per cent in some communities – have been prescribed anti-depressants at some stage of their lives. I simply do not believe that one in ten young men have the internal chemical imbalance that leads to depression.

I have worked with hundreds of patients who were suffering from depression. I always asked them what else was going on in their lives, if they were on medication and whether the medication was working. When I asked them what was happening, many told me they were not doing what they wanted and felt trapped in situations that really didn't work for them. When I speak to young men who have been diagnosed with depression time and again I hear that their situation at home and their relationship with one or both of their parents has broken down. They don't know what to do with their lives, they don't feel like they have any control, nor do they feel like they are seen for who they really are.

The main chemical in the brain that is involved with depression is serotonin. Chemical treatment of depression now tends to focus on increasing the available circulating levels of serotonin. However, exercise is also known to release serotonin (just ask any fitness fanatic what happens to their mental state when they stop for a few days). It has also been shown that when someone is doing what they love, what they are passionate about, or when they are in the company of people that they love, there's an increase in their circulating levels of serotonin.

I have come to believe, as I said earlier, that in many cases, depression is a 'sickness of the soul'. When a young man has no purpose, a troubled family situation, poor ability to relate to others, is unaware of his own gifts and talents, doesn't feel supported, believes that he has no control over his life, is still being treated like a boy and therefore struggles to see a future for himself, chances are he's is going to feel depressed.

A young man's PI wellbeing directly relates to his chances of getting depressed. If he scores well on the PI scale then through the relationships he has with his family and his friends, being physically healthy, exercising regularly, knowing what he is good at, and being passionate about the things he does – as well as being acknowledged and having men he can talk to if he has problems – then he is much less vulnerable to depression because he will be living the life that works best for him.

Peer pressure and the tyranny of marketing

Pressure from peer groups and from advertising and marketing is a major issue for young men today. Their friends will have a strong code of conduct which includes how they should dress, what music they should listen to, how they should talk, who they should hang out with, what they should be doing in their spare time, what sports they should play, and even which girls they should go out with.

More money is spent on market research every year than on any other form of research. Market research is designed to entice the target audience to buy the product the company is wanting to sell – regardless of whether it is good for them or something they truly need. In fact often it is exactly the opposite. Take, for example, the many types of energy drinks currently available. The message our sons get is that if they don't drink these beverages they are uncool and missing out because everyone else is, especially the great looking kids in the commercials. Marketing aims to convince our kids that drinking these drinks will give them the lifestyle that they see on TV.

Instead of a world where boys are encouraged to be themselves and to find their own inner truth and purpose in life, marketing would make every young man exactly the same. To get them to wear the same clothes, eat the same food, and have the same accessories. The ideal marketing campaign would result in all young men being clones and spending all their time and money identically so that the people who own the products can make more money, regardless of whether it is actually harmful to the health and wellbeing of our sons. It is hard to believe that they are willing to sacrifice the wellbeing and individuality of our boys just for their own financial gain.

Peer group pressure is another powerful force our sons will have to deal with. If a group of guys has been drinking and then gets into a car it can be very hard for your son to say no when they are all calling him a baby for not coming along for the ride.

A young man's PI score directly affects how he deals with this sort of pressure. If he is confident, feels supported, knows what he wants and has the sort of relationship with his parents where things are openly discussed, he is less likely to make a decision based on wanting the approval of others and will have the self-confidence to choose his own destiny. If he feels lost, out of control and unsure of his place in the world, then he is more likely to succumb to pressure from peer groups and from advertising and marketing.

For a young man's level of wellbeing to be as high as possible, the five factors on the PI scale all need to be addressed. In the few next chapters I will look at each factor individually and outline the specific things that both fathers and mothers can do to maximise them.

Key Points from Chapter 6

- Your son needs to develop a healthy Personal Identity

- Family relationships, key life skills, physical health, recognition of his gifts and talents and support through the transition from boy to young man make up a Personal Identity

- The influence of technology, drugs, alcohol, peer pressure and advertising will all be dependent upon his Personal Identity, as will his susceptibility to depression

CHAPTER 7

The critical father/son relationship

David is a fifty-one-year-old writer. 'The self-confidence I have from knowing I was loved by my father is one of the things that defines me. I think it's priceless. I've gone through life with a tremendous sense of self: I've felt blessed, wanted and enabled by his love. So there's very little disappointment. To this day, my father is proud of me and adores me and likes to be in my company. I think it's a really rare thing. I feel for boys or men who haven't had that. I see so many men bruised and battered emotionally more than physically by their fathers' seeming indifference or lack of attention. I have a lot of male friends in whom I can see the damage. Even as grown men, they are still longing for their father's approval and love, and I don't think they'll ever get it and it'll be a hole in their heart until the day they die. Even if they are able to turn it around and give it to their sons, it's not something that they would have ever known, because their fathers didn't know it, and going all the way back, for generations, men didn't know how to do that.'

Gerald, a businessman in his sixties, describes his relationship with his father. 'Having given up on a relationship with my father, and with other people, I became a loner and was determined to show them that I was better than everyone else. It manifested in anti-social behaviour, drinking, then drugs, and in my twenties, in making a lot of money and showing it off. I was still taking drugs every day until I was in my forties – nearly thirty years later. I smoked marijuana and drank heavily. They were masking the pain and loneliness and covering up the lack of connection to others, the sense of isolation. Even though I was married with two children, I was still not connected. I think the drugs kept me from being connected to my own family.'

Harvard psychologist William Pollack's research shows that one of the best things a boy can get when he is growing up is 'an extra dose of dad'. Pollack followed a group of boys for eleven years and concluded that, 'the more shared activities a boy had with his father, the more education he completed'. He also found that the closer the emotional bond between father and son, the lower the incidence of social delinquency.

Parenting expert Steve Biddulph suggests that a young man needs mutual love and respect with his father before he can truly become his own man. If this doesn't happen, he can be left with either an insatiable desire for personal power, or a destructively low self-esteem. Many will work obsessively accumulating wealth, power and status to fill a hole where their father's love should have been. Others end up trying to fill the hole with drugs, alcohol and other addictions. A strong and loving father/son relationship gives your son the best foundation he can have.

This is one of the most important points in this book. Boys need their fathers, but we are currently living in the most 'under-fathered' time in history. Dads spend an average of less than one hour a day with their sons. Often when they do they are on their mobile phone or distracted by other things. The boys too are often listening to their iPods or playing on mobile gaming devices. It's no wonder we are witnessing a crisis.

Dads need to make the time, be aware of how they are parenting and prioritise the wellbeing of their sons. It may not have been the case for you with your father, but that is not a valid excuse. Your boy needs you to be emotionally and physically available, to support him, to be honest about who you are and to help him become a young man with passion and a purpose in life.

Fathering young men is different from fathering boys

Raymond is sixty-eight and a builder. 'My son used to be my shadow when he was young. He would follow me into the workshop and ask me a million questions about what I was doing and how things worked. He used to cry when I went to work and would be sitting outside the carport sometimes when I came home waiting for me. I guess I was pretty strict but my father had been the same and it was the only way that I knew. By the time my son turned fifteen he was taller than me. He stopped coming to the workshop and we didn't talk much any more. He just seemed to spend all his time in his room. One day I heard him being rude to his mother and I told him to apologise. Things got out of hand and we ending up having a big fight. He actually punched me in the face and broke my nose. We avoided each other after that and about a year later he moved out. I don't think I saw or spoke to him for at least five years. Now he is thirty and we see each other at Christmas and things but he always seems really on edge. I've never talked to him about the fight we had, or about my father. Losing the relationship with my son is probably the saddest thing that has happened in my life.'

When your boy is young your fathering role involves mutual activities, having fun, teaching him the difference between right and wrong and showing him how to do things. My boys used to believe that I was some sort of Superman. They thought I could do anything and would follow me around and want to spend as much time as possible with me. When I'd come home from work they would run to the door and literally jump on me in their excitement. I was their hero.

When your son is a boy:

- You tell him what to do because you know best
- You make the rules and you are the boss
- You discipline him when he misbehaves
- You only tell him selected parts of your life story because he is too young to hear everything.

My, how things change!

There are some very necessary changes that have to happen in the father/son relationship as a boy becomes a young man. Like it or not, the relationship *will* change because your son is changing, and it can happen very quickly. Seemingly overnight, your son will:

1. No longer automatically accept everything you say as being true; he may even disagree with everything you say just because you are the one saying it

2. No longer see you as his hero, he'll likely start competing with you for the position of dominant male in the household (and even see you as a big idiot)
3. Not want you to tell him what he can and can't do; he will want to decide for himself
4. Form his own version of how life should be and not be wanting you to lecture him or tell him how to live.

What fathers need to do

When I give talks to parents, I often start by asking the dads in the audience what sort of relationship they want to have with their sons when they are adults, say when they're around thirty years of age. I give them a moment to think about it. Invariably, I hear the same thing. 'We want to be mates. We want to enjoy spending time together, to have an open, honest relationship, to share what is going on in our lives and support each other. We want our sons to *want* to spend time with us.'

The teenage years are when a father and son can build a new type of relationship. If they do it right, it will be the foundation of something that is lifelong and supportive. It is also when you run the greatest risk of losing your son for years or even permanently damaging your relationship. If you try to keep parenting a young man in the same way that you did when he was a boy, he will likely shut down, rebel and do everything he can to break away from you. He may never come back. There are three important things to do that will allow you to create a long-term, loving and supportive relationship with your son:

1. Bring him into your world and the world of men
2. Honour and recognise his gifts and talents
3. Create a shift in the balance of power.

Bring him into your world and the world of men

Share your stories

One of the best and most effective ways of bringing your son into your world is to share your life stories. I'm talking about the *real* stories, warts and all. When he was young you only told your son certain things and this was appropriate. Now if you truly want to end up as mates with a mutually respectful relationship, your son needs to know who you actually are. Telling stories is not about making you out to be a hero, it is about giving your son the opportunity to learn what is to be a man. Teenage boys want to know the real situations you have been in, they want to know what you did, they want to hear the outcomes and then they want to be able to ask questions. That is how they learn and how they work out for themselves the kind of man they want to be.

Of course you have to find the right time and do it in

the right way. It's not about saying, 'Well, when I was a boy …' and then telling him how tough you were. It's also not appropriate when you are in the middle of an argument or when he obviously doesn't want to listen because he is doing something else. There is an art to telling stories and a part of that is timing. It may be in the car when you are driving, it may be when you are relaxing after dinner, or it may be last thing at night. Be sensitive to whether it feels appropriate or not. You know you are doing it well when your son starts to ask questions and wants to hear more.

The stories must be the ones that had the most impact on you and changed your life. Your son has to hear not only about your successes and triumphs but also about where you struggled and the times that you feel you failed. Tell him how you dealt with adversity, where you made mistakes and how you handled the consequences. Allow him to ask questions and answer them as honestly as you can.

Sharing stories will deepen your relationship with your son, it is a great way for him to learn and it can also help clear up a lot of misunderstandings. Young boys construct their own versions of events. They make countless assumptions about your behaviour without the benefit of the full picture. They see themselves as the centre of the universe and therefore often blame them-selves for things such as a father's absence, or a family separation, and can come to the conclusion that they are unloved or unlovable. Hearing your perspective can transform your son's understanding. He will see that you are a real person with your own life, struggles, hopes and dreams. This will have an impact on how he relates to people and events, and his ability to respond to others with empathy and compassion.

Take him along when you spend time with your mates

I can't recommend highly enough including your son in activities you do with your male friends (unless of course all you do is go to the pub, in which case I suggest you find some other activities!). First of all, the other men will enjoy seeing and getting to know your son. You will notice older men instantly drop ten years in age as soon as a young man is in the room. They will be keen to talk to your son and find out what he is up to. They are likely to comment on things like how big or strong he is, how he resembles you or how good looking he is. They will be interested in his hobbies and how he is going at school, they may want to wrestle with him and they will certainly be looking to share stories with him about when they were his age.

Your son will see you in a new light. He will appreciate the camaraderie. He will feel proud to be with you and your friends and he will stand taller in their company. Even if he's struggling at the time, your friends will recognise and usually bring out the best side of him. He may not be so comfortable talking to you but he will likely enjoy talking to them.

Encourage your mates to talk about their lives. It is important that they tell the *real* stories and the ones that really shaped them.

• • •

Having spoken to hundreds of young men over the years, I know that most find being a teenager difficult and challenging. However, most also believe that they are doing it alone and that all of their friends find it easier than they do. When they hear the stories of their fathers and other men – how they struggled at the same stage, how life has not been all easy for them – this tells him that in spite of their current difficulties, they're going to be okay.

Sharing stories doesn't only teach young men about hardships. When young men hear stories of success and the things that adults create – the beautiful and special relationships that they can have with their partners, the possibilities that life holds – it inspires them to also want to succeed and realise their innate potential.

Honour and recognise his gifts and talents

Mark is fifty-eight and owns a successful sound recording studio. 'All I ever wanted to do was play music. From when I was a kid I always was singing or playing this or that musical instrument. I could play just about anything once I practised and could easily work out songs from the radio. My dad was a doctor and completely tone deaf. He couldn't even play the recorder and hardly ever listened to music, but to his credit he always supported me. For my twelfth birthday he bought me a drum kit and another year he bought me an amplifier. He used to take me to concerts and even be my roadie when I started playing in bands. I am so grateful he didn't try to force me into becoming a doctor or something. I've had an amazing life, made good money and until my dad died a few years back I can honestly say he was my best friend.'

Brent is fifty-two and divorced. 'As a kid I was passionate about anything artistic or creative. I spent hours making up theatre shows, writing music and putting on performances. Sometimes I did them for the dog and other times for anyone I could get to watch. It was what I loved doing the most and all that was important to me. I wanted so badly to be some type of performer when I grew up but my father kept on saying that my "artistic ways" were just a passing phase. He bullied me into becoming an accountant because he said people will always want help dealing with their money. Now I've spent nearly thirty years sitting at a desk dealing with other people's problems. Some of the guys at work love their job but I just hate it. I've made lots of money but I've always disliked being an accountant and I always will. I reckon that's why I started drinking heavily when I was in my twenties. I was so disappointed with the way that my life had gone that I turned to the bottle.'

Your son needs to know that you love him for who he truly is as opposed to feeling that he will get your love when he does what you want or becomes who you think he should be. Mark's dad supported him even though he probably understood very little about the world of music. He supported him because he could tell that this was what Mark really wanted to do. This was where his gifts lay and this was what he was passionate about.

Forcing your son into doing something he doesn't want to do, but that you want him to do, can result in serious, long-term problems.

Ultimately, loving him for who he is rather than what he does is what counts.

Enter your son's world

In the same way as you need to bring your son into your world, you need to enter your son's world. You need to spend time doing the things that really matter to him, things that he is interested in and passionate about. These may not be your favourite activities but your son needs to know that you are interested in him. If he loves playing soccer then go and watch him play, and when you can't, find out how he went in the game. If he is artistic then spend time looking at his creations and ask him to explain what he has been doing. Even if it is not something that you are into, explore the world your son lives in. He will really appreciate this. When you start to recognise your son's gifts and talents, make sure you tell him and acknowledge what you see.

Research has proven that young men whose fathers show them acceptance and support are happier and do better in school. They report lower levels of depression, anxiety and fewer behavioural problems. The young man who spends time with his father and knows he is loved, who feels valued for who he is and is aware that he will be supported to achieve the things he wants to, will have this as the background to his thoughts, feelings and actions for the rest of his life.

A father once told me that he was struggling to connect with his fourteen-year-old son who was now starting to get in trouble at school. I asked him what his son was interested in and he told me that all he seemed to want to do was play computer games. I asked him if they ever played computer games together and the dad told me that he thought they were a mindless waste of time and that he could hardly use a computer anyway. We talked for a while and I suggested to the dad that maybe he could ask his son to show him a bit about the games.

I saw that same father a couple of months later and asked him how he and his son were going. 'Great!' he told me. 'You wouldn't believe it, we play computer games together nearly every night and we both just love it. It has changed our whole relationship. We are talking again and having fun together. He has even been teaching me about computers and how to use them for my work. My son is also doing better at school and not getting into trouble. The change is amazing.'

Spend one-on-one time together with no interruptions

It is possible to be with your son but not really *be* with him at all. I have watched men take their sons to sport and then sit reading the paper or spend the entire time on their mobile phones looking in the other direction while their son is playing. In the car, which used to be a place to talk and share, dads can now be on their bluetooth mobile phones while their sons are in the back with headphones on watching a DVD.

A recent Australian survey of young people found that over one third ranked 'time' as the most important thing that they wanted from their parents. They also said that 'being listened to and understood' was a vital component of this 'time'. What's more, forty-one per cent of parents ranked 'spending more time' as the most important thing they would have done if they could do things over.

Making time to spend with your son one-on-one with no interruptions (mobile phones turned off) is a great way to build your relationship. He will realise he is important enough to get your undivided attention, which is something that young men crave from their fathers. Of course in this hectic world it is not always easy to find time. Dads' schedules are busy, and many young men also have full calendars with after-school activities, weekend sport, and so on. Time together may not be possible every day and it may not happen just because you want it to. It's something that you and your son need to plan together, which can also be part of the fun.

For some it is kicking the football in the park on a Saturday afternoon or going to the movies once a fortnight or playing chess or computer games in the evenings. For others it is crossing out in their diaries one or more weekends a year when they go away together. The key is that it is something that you both want to do and that it is a time when your two worlds become one.

My two sons are now in their twenties and living in college at their universities. We have a long-standing agreement that once a year we go on an adventure holiday together. Sometimes it is one-on-one and sometimes it is the three of us. We've been on road trips up the east coast and diving together on the Great Barrier Reef. I took my eldest son surfing in Papua New Guinea one year and my youngest camel riding in the desert another. It is a time that we all love, a time when we connect deeply and are able to talk about anything and everything.

Create a shift in the balance of power

A young boy looks to his father to learn what behaviour is acceptable. He looks to him for acknowledgement and comes to him with questions or problems. Young boys believe their fathers know pretty much everything and can do anything they want. A father will teach his son many things – from tying his shoelaces, to kicking a football to putting a hook on a fishing line. His role is also to set boundaries and teach his son what is okay and what is not.

If a boy oversteps the boundaries of what is appropriate behaviour then his father (along with his mother) will generally be involved in disciplining him.

The situation changes dramatically however when a boy reaches puberty and becomes a young man. Now it is time for dad to let go of being the all-powerful authority over his son. The new relationship must develop into one of respect for each other as individuals who both have their own opinions, ideas and ways of being in the world.

It is normal for a young man to start questioning his father as he seeks to establish his own individual identity. Dads need to really listen to what their sons have to say. A son must be able to challenge his father without destroying the relationship. A shift in the balance of power must take place in which a father relinquishes absolute control. They are now both men, and each individual's opinion must be heard and respected by the other. This will teach the young man an invaluable lesson – that power can be shared, and need not be fought over.

Unfortunately, many fathers feel threatened by their boys as they become young men. In the animal kingdom the dominant male would generally kick the young male out at this point. If he didn't want to go, the subsequent fight could easily end in injury or even death.

As a boy becomes a young man, it is natural for him to challenge his father. These days my sons regularly challenge me to competitions including push-ups, tennis and how far I can kick a football. I can see how much they want to win and what a big thing it is for them when they do. My youngest son, much to his own amazement, is now some 20 centimetres taller than me. He just loves the fact that he towers over me. He's forever coming up and standing next to me, patting me on the head (which drives me mad) and showing me how high he can reach or jump then asking me if I can do the same. It is as though he is continually looking to reinforce the fact he's taller not only in his mind, but in mine as well.

A young man will also challenge his father on an intellectual level. He wants to work things out for himself and will no longer automatically accept that what you say is right. Young men begin to question things and form their own opinions. They want to be heard and have their ideas given fair consideration.

When a boy becomes a young man he no longer wishes to be told what to do. He wants to be able to make his own choices. If you try to fight this he will just push back harder. Over time, you have to give your son increasing freedom to make his own decisions, but correspondingly he must learn that privileges are connected to responsibility.

It's so important that as role models we don't let our relationship degenerate into power plays. How our sons relate to us will influence how they relate to all men and situations that deteriorate into verbal or physical abuse can have disastrous effects. Abuse of any kind by a father destroys the self-esteem of the emerging young man. It sows seeds of doubt that can have profound lifelong consequences.

Shaming your son is the worst thing you can do

It is crucial to not shame a young man when he stumbles, makes a mistake, or oversteps boundaries. Shaming can destroy a young man's sense of wellbeing: it affects him at a very deep level and impacts his self-esteem. He no longer feels in control of his situation, he no longer feels capable, and worst of all he no longer feels loved. These feelings can be so debilitating that he will change his behaviour in order not to experience them again. This can crush his natural self-expression and confidence.

If your son tries something, doesn't succeed, and then is shamed, verbally abused or made to feel like he's a failure, there is a serious risk he will not be prepared to try it again in future. If, on the other hand, you support him, reflect on what happened, work out why it happened and give him positive feedback and praise for trying in the first place, he will feel safe and confident to have another go.

Why do fathers shame their sons? Most do it in order to control them and make them behave the way that they want. In the past, physical punishment was more commonly used to discipline boys and deter certain behaviours. These are examples of serious shaming. When a boy is beaten by a man he feels powerless, victimised and unloved.

> Richard is a sixty-five-year-old electrician. 'My dad used to have a leather strap that hung on the back of the kitchen door. If I misbehaved my mum would say, "Wait until your father gets home". I would hear the front door open and my dad coming up the stairs. Mum would talk to him and often I would run off and hide, but he always found me. I'd struggle but it was no use 'cause Dad was so much stronger than me. Sometimes he would hit me so hard that I would be sore for days. Afterwards I would go to my room, get under the covers and cry. I hated my mum and dad so much and I would dream about punishing them by running away and never coming back.'

Although physical punishment is now considered unacceptable and indeed illegal in many places, verbal punishment remains prevalent. Many men – often without even realising it – verbally shame their sons in order to regulate their behaviour. They say things like, 'You always do the wrong thing', 'You're acting like an idiot', 'You're a selfish brat', 'You're hopeless', 'Why can't you be more like so-and-so?', or 'None of the other boys behave like you'.

> Geoff is thirty-nine. 'I hate my father, nothing I ever did was good enough, he could always do it better. From the time I was a little kid I always remember him telling me I was useless. I used to love building things but if ever I showed him what I had done he would laugh and then point out everything wrong with it. It's had a big effect on my life. I always believe everyone else is better at things than me and if I ever have to show someone at work what I have been doing I get incredibly nervous, I start sweating and I feel sick. I am scared stiff they are going to criticise me. I avoid doing anything that could expose me to other people's opinions, which means I spend a lot of my time hiding and not doing what I really want.'

A boy who is repeatedly shamed will develop a shamed identity in which he thinks of himself as a bad, worthless person. Furthermore, he will imagine that others think of him that way, too. His self-esteem will plummet and this can give rise to feelings of depression, alienation, self-doubt, loneliness, inferiority, inadequacy, failure and helplessness.

In his writing on shame, American psychologist Gershen Kaufman says, 'Shame is the most poignant experience of the self by the self, whether felt in humiliation or cowardice, or in a sense of failure to cope successfully with a challenge. Shame is a wound felt from the inside, dividing us both from ourselves and from one another.'

Shaming might be initially painful but repeated shaming leads to a deadening of feeling, a kind of numbness in which part of a boy's personality closes down. Boys who are repeatedly shamed when they are young may work extra hard to please those who have shamed them but they often learn to hide things and become secretive when they are older. Shame can also lead to a fear of being exposed and can make boys withdraw from relationships. They may display contempt, superiority, bullying, and obsessive perfectionism. In some cases, boys who have been shamed will try to make themselves feel worthwhile by degrading others. This is a precursor to bullying and if this behaviour continues on into adult life a man may transfer it to his wife and children. Some men shame their sons because of their own insecurity and experience of having been shamed themselves.

Single fathers

Sadly, today many parents are separating which means that many fathers only see their sons some of the time. I was one of these fathers and I know first-hand how hard it can be. However, even if we are not living together with the mother of our children, and even if we are not with our kids seven days a week, we are still their fathers, we will always be their fathers, and our role is just as important as if we were living under the one roof. My family's living situation changed a number of times. Occasionally I had my boys full-time, sometimes they lived in another part of the country, and other times we had a shared arrangement. I certainly didn't do everything perfectly but I did the best that I could. These are some of the key things I worked out:

1. I always had a bedroom set up for my sons with their clothes, toys and sporting gear so that when they were with me they felt at home, not like guests. When they arrived I always tried to set up a routine as quickly as possible. That meant whether they were with me for a weekend or a month we just got on with it as if it were normal and we always lived together.

2. My boys really needed time with me when I wasn't distracted and could give them my full attention. They hated my mobile phone because it gave them the message that whoever was on the phone was more important then they were. They just loved it when we did things together, whether it was

playing at the park, going bowling, watching TV together or having a surf. After we had spent that time together they were much more relaxed about me getting on with my life. If we didn't spend that time then they started to misbehave.

3. I had to put the needs of my sons ahead of any of my own personal issues – which didn't come naturally, I assure you – including what was going on between their mother and me. What I mean by this is that I learned that arguing or fighting with their mother had a negative impact on the kids and so I made a decision to avoid it at all costs. I also made a promise to myself to never say anything bad about their mother in front of them.

4. I accepted that when they were not with me I had to get on with things and that when they were with me I had to give them priority. It felt like a double life at times but I believed that there was no point in being miserable when they weren't there and equally there was no sense in not being able to enjoy our time when we were together. They were never upset to leave and go back to their mother and they were always happy when it was time to be with me again. I discovered that at the airport there is an amazing phenomenon that happens at the end of school holidays. Peaking on the last day, increasing numbers of dads bring their children to catch planes back to their mothers. The men shuffle awkwardly while they wait, give their children furtive hugs and

kisses as they leave. Numerous times I watched my two boys walk across the tarmac to their plane while I stood there with tears in my eyes. They would be chatting away happily and never once did they turn back. I wouldn't want them to be any other way but it was always a long, lonely drive home.

5. I fed them the best and healthiest food I could get my hands on, encouraged them to spend lots of time outdoors, tried to minimise using the TV or computer as a babysitter, and told them I loved them at least once a day.

Gifts of a mentor

Dan is forty-two and runs a successful chain of gyms. 'Growing up I was fortunate to know an older man who also became a great friend, I guess you could call him a mentor. His name was Rene and he changed my life. He was the husband of my mum's best friend and we got on from when I first met him at about the age of nine. His face lit up whenever he saw me. He used to take me fishing in his boat which was my favourite thing to do. I could talk to him about anything and he always seemed to have an answer. We spoke for hours and he used to tell me stories about when he was growing up and all the adventurous things he had done.

'When I got older and things got a bit rough or I had a problem, I could ring him and we would head out in his boat or sit on his back porch for a chat. There were things I just couldn't talk to my mum or dad about but with Rene it was different. He never told me off or got angry with me, no matter what I had done. He never told me what to do but often after I'd talked to him I would know that I had to go and fix something up, apologise to someone, or make amends for something. I reckon I would have been in a lot of trouble if it hadn't been for Rene.

'I still see Rene even though he is in his eighties. I think he is the wisest man I have ever met. I can still talk to him about anything and I regard him as one of the men who has helped me the most in my life. I just hope that my sons have men like Rene in their lives.'

In Greek mythology, Mentor was the son of Alcumus and, in his old age, a friend of Odysseus. When Odysseus left for the Trojan War he placed Mentor in charge of his son, Telemachus. This ancient story is the source of the modern use of the word *mentor*, which means a trusted friend, counsellor or teacher.

A mentor is someone who, 'can reassure each child of his innate worth, instil values, guide curiosity, and encourage a purposeful life'. A mentor provides advice and support, watches over and fosters the progress of a younger, less experienced person.

A young man needs to learn from men who have experiences that are different to those of his father. In the past the role of a mentor was considered vital to the development of a young man. Indigenous societies understood that adolescent boys needed care and attention from the whole community, not just from their parents. Often a number of older men would be involved in the mentoring process, teaching the youngsters to hunt and fish, where to find water, how to make musical instruments and many other skills.

The mentors would also tell the young man stories about their community. They would pass on the knowledge and teachings that they had been taught. They frequently took charge of disciplining young men because they knew it was difficult for fathers, as the competitive element between the two would get in the way. There was a risk that if it was left to the father he could be too lenient, or indeed too harsh, as he was unable to make unbiased judgements.

As a boy becomes a young man he will look for recognition not only from his father, but from wider society. Many young men know that their fathers will either acknowledge them whatever they do, which diminishes the effect, or worse, they'll criticise them regardless of the effort involved. In some cases a father's acknowledgement becomes less fulfilling. A good mentor is someone who can give fair and just acknowledgement.

The young man will know that praise does not come lightly but he will also know that it will be given when it is due. The mentor gives the young man a realistic sense of how he is actually doing in the world.

The relationship between a mentor and a young man is not the same as that of a teacher and a student. Mentoring is concerned with the acquisition of life skills and of learning how to approach and deal with the situations that arise as a young man enters the world. Being a mentor is not a formal or defined role. It is about being a role model and being available when needed. Mentors give advice and support when asked, rather than stepping in and telling a young man how to live his life. A good mentor will answer questions with stories rather than direct answers.

Unfortunately, in modern society, many young men don't get mentored and if they do, it happens by chance. In some cases, those who mentor may not understand their role and may do it badly. While sports coaches, teachers, uncles and bosses can all be good mentors, in most cases men in these roles don't have the opportunity to develop the one-on-one special relationship that characterises the best mentoring.

A good example of mentoring is the old apprenticeship system. Traditionally, young men would spend four to six years working and learning a trade. They would not only acquire the skills necessary for the job but they would also learn valuable life lessons from the older tradesmen. Unfortunately, this is less common these days as a greater portion of the education for trades occurs in colleges and the one-on-one teaching that used to be the norm is now rare.

Mentoring is a privilege and a responsibility. Finding a good mentor is not easy. However, if you do have trusted friends or relatives who you respect and who get on well with your son, then encourage them to spend time together. Tell the man you feel he has the qualities that you would like to see in a mentor and ask him to consider taking on the role. If you can find a good mentor for your son you are giving him a great gift.

Many men don't understand what it is to be a mentor but most will remember another man who was there for them when they were growing up. You may have to explain that you are looking for a man to support, acknowledge and encourage your son in ways that are outside of what you as his father are able to do. A mentor may come from within your existing close networks and could be an uncle, a godfather or close family friend.

A warning about mentoring

There is a power associated with being a mentor and occasionally this power can be abused. The worst and most tragic cases come in the form of child abuse. Men who have younger men or boys in their care and then choose to sexually, physically, emotionally or verbally abuse them are perpetrating a heinous crime that resonates throughout society. These men, who are a small minority, destroy the invaluable and necessary gift of mentoring. They make it increasingly difficult for good men to mentor.

Many older men who are keen to spend time with young men are looked upon suspiciously. I recently heard a story of a retired mechanic whose children had left home and had children of their own. Most days this man worked on his motorbikes in the back of his house with the door to his garage open. A boy who used to walk by on his way home from school stopped and watched one afternoon. Eventually he began asking questions about the bikes and what the man was doing. Each afternoon the boy would stop by and the pair would talk. The boy lived at home alone with his mother, had no male role models and was obviously enjoying the opportunity to be in a garage surrounded by motorbike parts and 'boys' toys'.

Aware of the growing interest the boy had in what he was doing, the man suggested he tell his mother and invite her over so that they could meet.

The next morning an angry and worked-up mother stormed through the door of the man's garage and told him, in no uncertain terms, that if he *ever* spoke to her son again she would call the police. 'I don't want my son around men the likes of you!' she said and left before the man could even say a word. That boy never returned and a perfect mentoring opportunity was lost.

A generation of young men is missing out on the gifts on offer from older men because of the crimes of a few. At the same time, a generation of older men is missing out on the gift of being a mentor. Trust in men has been damaged. The man in the previous story had so much to offer and was genuinely looking forward to passing on his knowledge. We have an obligation to find ways to rebuild trust so that mentoring can once again become a part of our communities.

Key Points from Chapter 7

- The father/son relationship is so important and has to evolve when your boy becomes a young man

- Bring your son into your world

- Honour and recognise his gifts and talents

- Create a shift in the balance of power

- Mentors are a great support for your son

CHAPTER 8

The special mother/son relationship

This chapter is difficult for me to write. As a man, I have not experienced directly the special bond between a mother and her son. I have however spoken to many mothers and observed many different interactions. I'm also the very lucky son of an incredible woman who gave me all the love in the world and would do anything for me. Even so, Mum and I certainly had our struggles when I was a teenager! Neither of us really knew how to deal with what was going on. The love never wavered, but at a certain point in my teenage years I stopped communicating and began living a secret life. I realise that this was a difficult time for Mum because we had always been so close. With what I know now, I appreciate just how different things could have been.

I have sought the advice of a number of women in writing this chapter including friends, professional colleagues and of course, my mother. I have also included a few more real-life examples of mother/son relationships in order to cover the range of experiences.

A beautiful bond

Paul is a forty-seven-year-old clothing manufacturer. 'My mother was an incredibly important person in my life and we loved each other very much. When we were little she did everything for us kids. She cooked, cleaned and washed our clothes. She took us to school, picked us up and was a taxi driver all over town on the weekends. Being one of four boys and now having children of my own, I can't believe how hard she worked and yet she always seemed happy and there was lots of love and laughter in our house.

'When I became a teenager, she treated me very differently. She stopped telling me what to do and instead we used to spend hours in the kitchen talking about all sorts of things. She became my confidant. I could talk to her about whatever I wanted and she helped me explore lots of things that were going on. It's funny because in one way she pulled back from me and our relationship changed but in another way we became closer than ever.'

Gary, a forty-year-old businessman, describes his relationship with his mother. 'My mum tried to cling on just by doing things like making my bed, going into my room and tidying it, hassling me about what clothes to wear and to brush my hair. She just did all that because that's how she showed me that she loved me, but I didn't like it. I thought she just treated me like a little kid ... She didn't empower me to take responsibility for my own life and just kept on doing everything so I abused it and just let her do it, until I'd get irritated and tell her to piss off. It was just a really difficult time, we had no knowledge of what was happening and that I was changing and so we just pretty much turned on each other. When I moved up the coast I didn't speak to her for two years because she was still trying to tell me what to do.'

A mother and her son have a special and wonderful relationship. It is her eyes he looks into first, her that he smiles for and her that he cuddles when he is tired, hungry or afraid. A mother will know a lot about her son, from how he feels to what he wants to eat and when he needs to go to the toilet. Boys tell their mums everything. Mothers are finely tuned in to the needs, moods and personalities of their sons.

Every young boy should be lucky enough to have a loving, caring, nurturing mother. It's an important role.

If denied a mother's love as a child, a man may struggle with feelings of abandonment and low self-esteem.

Mothering boys is different from mothering young men

Nicky, a forty-two-year-old single mother, has an eight-year-old boy. 'My son lives like he is a little prince. I can't believe what I do for him. I am up before him and when he wakes I make him breakfast and put out his clothes for the day. I drive him to school and he takes a lunch I have made for him. I pick him up from school and have afternoon tea ready. He tells me absolutely everything he has done all day but never once has he ever asked me what I did with my day. Then he plays and watches TV until dinner. After he has eaten and left his dishes on the table I run a bath for him. I wash the dishes and tidy up while he is in the bath and then when he has finished his bath he stands up and I rub him down with a towel until he is dry, wrap it around him and send him to his bedroom. He drops his towel on the floor and puts on his pyjamas, which I place under his pillow when I make his bed in the morning. Then I read him a story until he is starting to drop off to sleep. I give him a kiss, turn off the light and quietly leave the room. I

have no idea where he is going to ever find a
wife that will do all of that for him.'

When your son is a boy:

- You do everything for him and he expects that and
may even treat you like you are his servant
- He tells you everything that is going on for him with
his friends, his feelings and his bodily functions
- If he gets angry he will often have a temper tantrum
and may hit you and tell you that he hates you
- He wants you to watch him all the time and tell
him how wonderful he is
- You are incredibly protective and your biggest
priority is to keep him safe.

The reality is that when a boy starts becoming a young
man, the mother/son relationship *must* change so that it
can stay strong and healthy through the transition from
boyhood to manhood. If the relationship can adapt, it
will remain loving and will bring both of you great joy
throughout your lives. Your son will live his own life and
you will be able to live yours knowing that you are each
there for the other when needed. It will be a relationship
based on respect and healthy communication.

It is crucial that both mother and son understand and
honour this so that the mother doesn't end up feeling
rejected or the son doesn't become suffocated as he
struggles for his freedom.

For many mothers it is challenging letting go of their baby. Many mums wish for him to remain their beautiful little boy forever. You may well love doing everything for him and knowing everything about him. It is a beautiful and special relationship and it is normal to not want it to end. Many mothers worry about how their son will cope out in the big bad world. It is normal to want to continue protecting him and that is certainly easier to accomplish if he is still your little boy.

Imagine a relationship with a young man who just throws his clothes on the ground when they are dirty or demands food when he is hungry. Imagine if this person who is now physically bigger than you has a temper tantrum every time he doesn't get what he wants or, worse, uses physical intimidation or violence when he's unhappy.

In the same sense imagine him telling you absolutely everything about his life. He will be discovering and exploring his emerging sexuality and developing intimate relationships. For this he needs to have his own private space. There is still plenty he can talk to you about and hopefully he can come to you when he wants advice or help, but he now must be the one to choose when to do so.

Working together, you can build a new and loving connection based on mutual respect that will support you both through your adult years. The degree to which you and your son are able to successfully evolve your relationship will also impact how he relates to his partners and other women in his life.

If the relationship **doesn't** evolve ...

Forty-six-year-old Isabella says, 'It was such a difficult and challenging time. I loved doing everything for my son Oscar. I adored the intimacy, the kissing and having him come into bed for cuddles in the morning. He was the most special thing in my life and I never wanted it to change. Then all of a sudden he didn't want to hold my hand when we were in the street, he wouldn't let me kiss him when I dropped him off at school, he stopped coming into my bed in the morning and he started locking the door when he was in the shower. Worst of all we used to talk every afternoon when he came home and he would tell me absolutely everything that he had done. Now he didn't want to do that any more and he even seemed angry when I asked him. I had this terrible feeling that my gorgeous boy was rejecting me.'

If the relationship between a mother and her son doesn't evolve, one of a number of things may happen. Your son may well:

- Become angry
- Withdraw
- Remain infantile
- Get depressed.

Patsy is thirty-nine. 'My son swears at me all the time. He is so much bigger than me now and I am scared of him. Recently when I told him to tidy his room things escalated into an argument and he shouted back at me, "What's your problem? Have you got your period or something? F^#k off or I will hit you!" It was terrible and made me feel totally sick and scared of my own son.'

If you try to maintain the relationship as it was when your teenager was a boy, it is likely your son will stop communicating, become angry or even physically violent.

Mothers often tell me they just don't understand what has happened to their once placid boys. They're hostile and won't talk or help out in any way.

I remember one mother bringing her son in to see me in my doctor's surgery. She sat between me and her sixteen-year-old son and proceeded to tell me how worried she was. Meanwhile her son sat there, visibly uncomfortable, with a baseball cap pulled down low over his eyes. His mother went on about how she didn't understand what had happened to her son and how there must be something wrong with him. Every time I tried to ask the boy a question his mother answered for him. To my amazement, at one point she even pulled a tissue out of her sleeve, licked it and went to wipe something off his face! I could see his growing discomfort as he opened and closed his fists and tapped his foot on the floor. Finally, I thanked the mother and asked her to leave the room so that I could talk to her son alone. She was hesitant but I gently guided her to the door and back out to the waiting area.

I turned around to see a different young man sitting on the chair. He had pushed his hat up and was instantly engaged. 'She drives me mad!' he told me. 'I never get any space, she wakes me up in the morning, puts my clothes out for me like I'm a baby and is always worrying about me. I'm sixteen, but I feel like I'm being suffocated. I know she loves me but I am so angry with her and I just want to run away and live somewhere else where I don't have to deal with her.'

Many young men simply shut down from their mothers at this time in their lives. They stop talking, stop sharing and stop being affectionate. For many mums, it feels like their sons no longer love them.

Felix is a thirty-two-year-old musician. 'For me it became like a survival exercise. I was just waiting for the time when I could leave home. I ignored my mother for years because she drove me crazy with all her mothering stuff and continued to treat me like I was five. I reckon for a while there I actually hated her. I wasn't rude and I didn't get angry, I just went into my own world and she wasn't part of it. If she asked me a question I'd give her the shortest answer possible before going to my room. I knew it was hurting her but to be honest I didn't care, and besides I think I believed it was her fault.

'I'm not sure if we ever got over that time. Sure, we talk a lot more and we are a lot closer, but as soon as she tries to start mothering me or fusses over me I just shut down again and have to get away. I don't know if that will ever change.'

Another possibility if the relationship doesn't evolve is that your son will remain infantile in his behaviour for far longer than he should. He will still need you to do everything for him and may become afraid to spend time away from home and try new things. He may only feel safe when he is at home or in your presence. He may have difficulty making friends and while he may be loving and affectionate at home it can be a compensation for what he knows he is missing out on in other parts of his life.

As your son and his friends' lives change, so must the way you treat him. If it doesn't, it will result in serious psychological discomfort which he will find it very hard to deal with. The world is telling him that he should be a man but his mother who knows him best is telling him that he is still a boy.

The impact on a young man's future relationships with women

'When I was young I wanted to marry my mother.'

For many men, including me, this statement will no doubt ring true. The way a man relates to his mother greatly influences the way he relates to other women. She is the first woman he knows and the woman that he spends the most time with during his formative years. If a man is still seeking mothering, then he may well look for the same thing in a partner. Women have told me that while they are prepared to mother their sons, they become frustrated and even angry when their husbands or partners expect similar treatment. They feel that their partners are looking for replacement mothers and are unable to meet them emotionally as independent equals. Unfortunately, this is a common occurrence.

Lee is fifty-nine and has been married to Jim for thirty-five years. 'It is a sad fact that my husband is really still a boy. He only thinks about himself and he always needs me to tell him how great he is. We were young when we got married and I think what he really wanted was a mother: someone to cook for him, clean his clothes and keep the house tidy. And that's what I have been doing all these years. It would be okay if he also thought about me, but it all just seems to go one way. He chooses what we watch on TV, he stays late at work or has a drink with the guys and doesn't even bother to let me know, he comes home at whatever hour and just sits down at the table expecting dinner to be ready. I've thought about leaving but the tragic thing is that I really don't know if he would cope without me.'

A young man must leave the bosom of his mother and learn to relate to women equally and respectfully as fellow adults. If he doesn't, he may forever relate to them in a dependent and immature way. Alternatively, he may be afraid of commitment due to his fear of and aversion to being mothered and controlled.

Michael, a teacher, talks about his mother, 'I don't think my mum ever let go ... being a mother was such a big part of her identity. I went overseas for a long time and when I came back there was a lot of fighting. We argued every time we were together; I'd love to say that didn't have to happen. My mother was so hard to break away from because she was so determined to keep the mother/son type connection going. I think she needed it for her sanity and she needed it for her sense of self, which was very fragile ... Sometimes it's hard for me to stay in relationships with women without feeling like I'm getting trapped and that I'll never get away. That's my particular piece of hell to deal with.'

If a man has never properly learned how to relate to women, and he reacts to his partner as he did to his mother when he was a child, there is a far greater risk of domestic violence. A five-year-old having a temper tantrum and hitting his mother or telling her he hates her is one thing, but a fully grown man losing his temper when he doesn't get his own way and being physically or verbally violent is both unacceptable and criminal.

I often hear stories of adult men who, in the presence of their own mothers, revert to feeling like and acting as though they are about twelve. Many tell me that their mothers still treat them like children, fussing around them and driving them crazy. Some of these men will get angry with their mothers and yet still seek acknowledgement from them.

Disastrously, men sometimes put their mother's needs before their wife's or their partner's, and end up caught in the middle trying desperately to please both. If a man has not separated emotionally from his mother, it can create a competitive relationship between her and his partner.

Kaitlin is fifty-two and separated from Anthony after ten years of marriage. 'I travelled halfway across the world to marry this fabulous man who I was in love with. But I didn't know I entering into a threesome. His mother rang him practically every day and I know that he talked to her about our problems. It made me furious. He said that he wanted to be with me but I could see he was totally afraid of doing or saying anything that would upset her. She always put on this sweet face when we were together, but behind my back I know she was trying to undermine me. Nothing I ever did was good enough for her precious son. And the worst part was that he never stood up for me. I don't know who I was more glad to see the back of when we separated, him or his mother.'

In one African country, boys are told a story when they are taken away to be initiated. At the end of the story the initiate has to make a decision between the young woman he has met in the story and his mother. Stories are used as a way of teaching and passing on knowledge. They are saying a man needs to choose who is going to be the number one woman in his life – but he can't have both. If he chooses his mother then he will not be able to have a proper relationship with another woman. If he chooses his wife or partner, then his relationship with his mother has to change.

What does the new relationship look like?

Here's the really great news. Your new mother/son relationship will:

- Empower him to become a healthy young man and increase his wellbeing on the PI scale
- Free you as a woman to pursue other things you love
- Create a strong connection that will last your whole lives.

This new relationship is based on respect and healthy, open communication.

Respect between a mother and her son

Respect means your son:

- Sees you as a real person having a life and needs of your own, not just being there for him
- Contributes in whatever way possible to looking after his own needs and those of the family
- Becomes aware of and can control his emotions so that if something doesn't go his way he doesn't sulk or have a temper tantrum
- Starts making his own decisions based on what he believes is true and fair rather than relying on you to decide everything for him.

Respect means you as his mother:

- Acknowledge your son is no longer a little boy and that he is ready to start exploring the world
- Give him space to make his own decisions and don't try to rescue him
- Don't accept rude or inappropriate behaviour
- Don't do everything for him
- Create healthy boundaries and let him know that you have your life to live too.

Healthy, open communication

Healthy, open communication means that:

- Your son now chooses what he talks to you about rather than just telling you everything
- Your son feels safe to discuss things with you that may be uncomfortable but for which he needs advice without fear of being judged. For example, what to do when other kids are drinking or taking drugs
- You are there to listen and support, not tell your son how to live
- You accept that your son has a private life and there are things that he won't talk to you about
- You can be honest and open about your own life and tell him your stories.

When you have a relationship that is based on respect and healthy communication everything changes. You will have more time and space to do what you want because your son will be looking after himself. He will be helping out where he can rather than expecting and waiting for you to do everything. He will be more responsible and you will be able to relax and know that he is thinking about his actions and their consequences. He will also not be looking to you to rescue him and will start finding ways to deal sensibly with his own problems.

Healthy communication will mean that while your son may not tell you everything, he'll know that you are there when he really needs you and that you are someone he can turn to and trust. You may hear things you don't want to hear, you may be asked questions you are not comfortable answering, but you need to move through this and be the one your son knows he can turn to.

This is also a time when you can share more about your life. There will be things he will know about you that you have already told him when he was young but obviously it has not been appropriate to share everything. Now is the time to tell him not only about how you grew up and what you did, but also where you struggled and what you learned along the way. As he begins to see you more as your own person you will find that a new level of love and respect will emerge between you.

If you take these steps, your relationship with your son will grow and remain healthy throughout your adult years. It can be engaging and strong without being needy. It will allow other people to enter your son's life without it becoming a competition for his love and affection. You will not be a threat to his wife or partner because you will respect his space and their boundaries. You will be welcomed into his future family and receive great joy from being a part of his life, while also being supported by him to live your own life to the fullest.

Single mothers

More and more women are finding themselves in the role of single mum. In addition, the father of their children is only partly present, may have a new partner and children, or may not be in the picture at all. This is challenging, especially when a mother then feels she has to take on the role of being both mother *and* father. I have worked with many single mums. I have seen the amazing job they do and the struggles they go through to be everything they can for their boys.

After hundreds of case studies, interviews and personal observations, I have come to the following conclusions with regards to single mums:

- Boys and young men *need* to spend time with their dads
- Try to work together with his dad in how you parent
- Never speak badly about his dad in front of him
- Don't compare your son's behaviour to his dad's

- Never use your son as a bargaining chip or a weapon against his dad
- If dad is not around, find other good men
- Look after your own health and wellbeing.

Your son will love his dad whoever he is. He will want to spend time with him and feel his love and acceptance. As parents, even if you're separated, both mum and dad can still support each other, openly communicate about your son and maintain consistent methods.

Naturally, it's more complicated if the relationship between you and your son's father has soured. You may be angry with him or he may be angry with you. There may be new partners involved, your separation may have been ugly and unpleasant, money and child support is usually stressful, your ex may have very different ideas about parenting and live a lifestyle that you don't approve of, or you may simply have come to the conclusion that you really don't like him.

Most of the above is irrelevant if you ask yourself the question, 'What is best for my son?' Despite what you may think, research confirms that the healthiest thing for your son is to have the best possible relationship with his dad. To have this, they need to spend time together and you need to support this. It also means trying to find ways to work together and communicate about your son's upbringing and his wellbeing.

It doesn't mean that you have to like his father or respect him. You don't actually have to have much interaction or communication with him other than with regards to your son. However, if you want to be able to positively influence the way his father parents and the quality of that parenting, the better you can communicate with him the more it will help.

Michael is twenty-eight. 'My mum and dad separated when I was twelve. There had been a lot of fighting and then Dad left. Not long after we found out that he had another girlfriend and they were living in a really nice house. Mum was so angry and wouldn't even let me go to visit him. She used to spend hours on the phone in the kitchen talking to her friends about what an arsehole my dad was and how he had ruined our lives. She was also always going on about how we had no money and that Dad had taken it all and was spending it on his new girlfriend. I was also so angry with my dad and I hated him. I used to cry sometimes at night in bed. Eventually, Dad took Mum to court so that he could see me. The first time he came to pick me up I was scared and I thought he would be mean to me and want to hit me or something. He stood at the door and was crying. He gave me a hug and wouldn't let me go. I didn't know what to do. I felt so confused. My mum always hated when I spent time with Dad. She was always angry when I came home and I never told her that I had a good time or she would get even more upset. I used to build model planes and the day I told her that I wanted to go and live with my dad she went into my room and broke every single one.'

One of the worst things a mother can do is speak badly about her son's father in front of him. Equally bad is using him as a weapon to get back at his dad. Regardless of how angry or disappointed you are, when your son hears you disparage his father it creates an enormous issue for him. He loves both of you and now he feels that he has to take sides. He is in a no-win position.

You should also avoid comparing your son to his father – *unless* it's in a positive light. The problems and issues that led to his father being absent are not your son's fault. They are *not* the same person. If you have lost respect and/or love for his father and then start comparing your son to him, your son will believe that he to is not worthy of love and respect. Once again, this only encourages a negative, confusing and destructive mindset. It may make you feel better at the time, but it is not helpful for your son.

If your son's father is not around, then find other good men to positively influence him. Uncles, grandfathers, partners, family friends, sports coaches or even teachers can all help. If they care about your son and are prepared to support him it will make a big difference to his health and wellbeing. Remember though that these men are going to be the role models. Choose carefully and take the process seriously. Think about what qualities you admire in a particular man. Consider whether he'll be able to give your son regular time and whether he is the sort of person you want your son to be able to ask for advice. Make sure you fully discuss the situation with the man in question.

Finally, it's really important you take care of yourself! You must stay as healthy as possible – if you don't, nobody will benefit. Too many single mums work so hard and make so much effort that they are constantly exhausted and lose themselves in the process. I know that it comes from a place of love and caring, but it's hard to be loving and caring when you feel rundown.

Ensure you have your own regular special time to do what *you* want. Keep in contact with your friends. Exercise and eat as well as you can. Your son won't care whether the house is spotless but he will appreciate it when you are happy and have energy to laugh, play and do things together.

Remember, your son loves you and wants to have the best relationship possible with you.

Key Points from Chapter 8

- Your relationship with your son has to change when he becomes a young man

- You have to stop mothering him and let him live his own life

- You can create a new relationship based on respect and healthy, open communication

- When you change the relationship with your son it will free you up to pursue your own passions

- Single mums need to support their boys so they can spend time with their dads

CHAPTER 9

The key life skills your son needs

By the time your son leaves home he needs certain life skills that will enable him to function well in the world and form healthy, long-term relationships. These skills directly affect his wellbeing on the PI scale. If he doesn't acquire these skills – for whatever reason – he is likely to struggle. Some skills will be learned at school, like socialising, mathematics and reading. Others will be learned at home – mostly from watching how you live your life. Remember, as parents or carers what you *do* is just as important as what you *say*. Here are a few basic life skills you can help your son with:

- Cooking and cleaning: he should be able to look after himself on a basic level with cooking, and cleaning his own clothes and living space
- Financial planning and management: we live in a world dominated by money and to have the skill to make a budget, plan ahead and save when necessary is invaluable
- Conflict resolution: inevitably, conflict will arise in personal and professional situations. If your son

is able to listen and understand another person's point of view, clearly articulate his own and then negotiate an outcome he will avoid a lot of grief.

While to most adults these sorts of skills will (hopefully) be commonplace, they may well be challenging for your son. That's because as a young boy he probably:

- Expected things but did not feel he had to do anything in return
- Was uninterested in what was happening in your life, or anybody else's except his own
- Lost his temper when he didn't get what he wanted
- Cried and acted like the world was about to end, or gave up if something didn't work out for him
- Thought of himself, ignoring the needs of others.

As a young man, these attitudes and behaviours *must* change. Apart from the general capabilities like cooking and cleaning and managing money, five vital life skills your son should have by the time he's ready to leave home are:

1. Understanding that privileges are connected to responsibility
2. Resilience if things don't go his way
3. High EQ, SQ and GQ (I'll explain these later)
4. The ability to find creative solutions to problems
5. Understanding the power of collaboration.

Understanding that privileges are connected to responsibility

Recently, a mother told me about her fifteen-year-old son who had been invited to a party. She was worried there would be older kids and alcohol at the party and she didn't want him to go. The young man of course was desperate to go and they had been arguing for hours. We discussed the fact that if she refused to let him go then there was a fair chance that some time in the future he would sneak off without her knowing.

I suggested they sit down together and negotiate the conditions under which he would be allowed to go to the party. In this case he had to do all his homework for the week, keep his room tidy and do all his jobs around the house – without arguing! They agreed on how he would get to the party and when he would come home. He agreed not to get a lift with any of the kids, nor to come home drunk (or in the back of police paddy wagon). He agreed that his mum could ring the parents of the kid having the party to ask about parental supervision. He agreed to take his mobile phone and to call if he was going to be late by even five minutes.

> His mum rang me the next week delighted and
> amazed that not only had her son agreed to the
> conditions beforehand, he did everything he
> said, was home on time and gave her a big hug
> and a kiss when he walked in the door.

As your son becomes a young man, one of the most important things you can teach him is that *privileges come with responsibilities*. As he wants more freedom to be able to do things like going out at night, he needs to accept that he must be appropriately responsible or he will lose the privilege.

All too often I have seen parents threatening their boys that if they don't behave or if they don't do what they are told then they won't get to go somewhere on the weekend, or they won't get pocket money, or they won't get to stay up and watch TV. And then despite not having done what their parents have asked them, the boys still get what they want. This sets up a terrible loop where the boy feels like he is entitled to everything but doesn't have to behave responsibly or do anything in return. This scenario is not healthy and it's certainly not the way the world works.

It is great to give your kids privileges and we are lucky that there are so many opportunities for them in this day and age. However, it cannot just be a one-way street. If your son wants to go to a movie on the weekend and you are paying and driving him there, then why shouldn't he do a few things around the house to help out in return?

And if he refuses, I recommend you don't take him to the movie. If he wants to learn the guitar and you are paying for the lessons then it is reasonable that he practises a few times a week and is on time for his lessons. If he doesn't, stop paying for his lessons. We don't do our sons any favours if everything is delivered to them on a silver platter and nothing is expected in return.

Parents decide what is fair and reasonable for a young boy but young men *must* be involved in the decision making process. When done properly this empowers them because they are not being controlled, they are being given choices and they are free to make their own decisions within a framework they have helped to build.

Pocket money is a good way to connect privileges with responsibility. Make an agreement with your son about the weekly jobs that he will do and if necessary write it down so it is there clearly for all to see. At the end of the week sit down with your son and work out exactly what he did and use this to determine what percentage of his pocket money he gets. Making a contract like this can help to take the emotional heat out of the negotiation. The chances are that you will see an increase in what gets done and, even better, you won't have to chase him to do it.

Some people are uncomfortable linking money with work around the house but consider the consequences of a young man *not* learning this lesson while he's at home. Society doesn't pay those who don't work (unemployment benefits notwithstanding). If your son wants to buy a car, a nice house and take holidays, he will have to work, be responsible and deliver on what he says. If he doesn't he will either not get paid or will get fired from his job – this is another of life's basic lessons.

Taking you, the parent or carer, 'out of the loop' is important. Instead of arguing or trying to force your son to do things, talk and negotiate beforehand. Once you agree, then it is up to your son whether or not he gets what he wants. You no longer constantly have to make and redefine the rules or be the enforcer. Now, if he does the responsible thing and keeps his word he gets the privilege. It's clear and simple.

As your son grows older, these discussions will become more serious as his privileges increase. At the same time, his responsibilities should increase *in equal measure*. At some stage, for example, he will get his driver's licence and no doubt will want to borrow your car. This is a big privilege and obviously he has to behave responsibly. The important thing here is that you both agree what he has to do if he is going to use your car. If he doesn't do what is agreed then he doesn't take your car. If he does then next time he knows that after a discussion about the conditions he will be allowed to take it again. The decision is one that he makes himself through his actions and his ability to take on and deliver on responsibility.

Resilience if things don't go his way

Andrew, age sixty-seven, is a successful entrepreneur. 'I had an amazing relationship with my dad. Looking back on life and my male friends I think I was definitely one of the lucky ones. My dad always encouraged me to try things. He used to say, "It doesn't matter if you don't succeed, son, just have a go." I remember building my first billy cart, the wheel fell of halfway down the hill and I crashed into a fence. Dad sat with me for hours and we took the whole thing apart, talked about it and worked out what went wrong. Then he helped me rebuild it and walked up hill with me. I can still hear him cheering as I made it to the bottom in one piece.'

George is a forty-four-year-old executive. 'My parents would take us on holidays and I remember my father wanted us to water ski. If we didn't get it the first time then we'd get abused and shamed. As this kept going on, I started to step back from everything we did. I was afraid to try anything because if you didn't get it right you were useless, you would be shamed in front of everybody else, and in front of your friends. To this day I struggle to try new things even when I know that I really should.'

It is crucial our sons know that if they try something and don't succeed at first that it's okay. Did you ever fail the first time you tried something new? This is a basic part of learning and growing. George from the story above doesn't try new things because he's petrified of failing. He is at risk of remaining stuck doing things he doesn't want to and living a life that doesn't work and is unfulfilling for him.

We need to teach our sons that we all get it wrong and we all make mistakes. The important thing is that we have a go and that we learn our lessons so that we don't make the same mistake next time. That is how we develop as human beings. It is an important part of building a good sense of wellbeing and a healthy Personal Identity. Being a man is not about succeeding every time!

Encourage your son to try things that he is interested in. If something doesn't work out then don't be hard on him but talk to him about what happened, how he could do it differently, and suggest that he has another go. Share your stories of when things didn't go right for you. Your son needs to understand that everyone fails sometimes – even you – but that is only part of what it takes to succeed in the long run.

Helping your son build resilience will really strengthen your relationship. When he fails at something he probably won't feel very good about himself. When he finds that you didn't judge him but instead are prepared to support him to work through the problem or have another go, he will feel a strong emotional connection as you have been there for him.

High EQ, SQ and GQ

When I was at school in the 1970s there was a lot of talk about how clever a person was based on his or her IQ. The letters stand for Intelligence Quotient. Through a series of tests that examined your mathematical and logical problem solving abilities, teachers were able to measure and give each person a score. A score of 100 was considered the average. If you scored over 160 you were ranked in the top two per cent of the population and were eligible to join an 'IQ society' called Mensa which meant that you could practise solving even more complex problems. IQ predominantly involves using the left side of the brain where not surprisingly our mathematical and logic-solving functions are located.

Then someone with a different sort of intelligence realised what many women have known forever – just because a man is good at maths and building things does not necessarily mean that he's smart! In fact he may still be a total idiot in many ways. Psychologists found there was a type of intelligence called EQ – Emotional Intelligence – which rates a person's emotional abilities. EQ defines how well someone relates to other people, whether they have empathy, and how aware they are of their own emotional state and the impact of what they do on others. So for example, someone who loses their temper when something goes wrong and blames everyone else might have a low EQ, as would someone who is unaware or uninterested in how other people feel and just thinks about themselves. EQ predominantly involves the right side of the brain where the more creative and emotional functions are located.

After IQ and EQ had been identified, there was a feeling in the medical world that human intelligence had been defined and that was the end of the story. Then someone came up with a different sort of intelligence again – SQ or Social Intelligence. Social Intelligence refers to one's ability to have awareness and insight, and to take into account what is happening in the field – in the bigger picture. An example of SQ would be if you are talking with a good friend and you are aware that they are sad as this is the anniversary of someone in their family having died. So not only is it appropriate to be gentle with them but it also may be a good idea to see if there is any way that you can support them or their family at this time.

Recently yet another type of intelligence has been named – GQ or Generational Intelligence. GQ involves the acquisition of intelligence and knowledge from previous generations and the passing on of that intelligence and knowledge to future generations. A person with good GQ will want to and be able to learn from the experiences of others. They won't be someone who believes that they have to work everything out for themselves and be dismissive of what others have to say.

Additionally, a person with a high GQ will be good at teaching and supporting those who are younger and less experienced so that they to can grow and perform well.

Sadly, we live in a society with increasingly poor GQ. Too many older people are not listened to or respected. More and more young men think that they know it all and have little to learn from the thousands of years of human experience that precede them. They take this attitude and belief into their adult years. We now know that certain behaviours are detrimental, like working really long hours; believing that money will bring happiness (and more money will bring more happiness); never seeing your children, and then just expecting to have a great relationship with them when they grow older. And yet generation after generation of men repeat the same mistakes.

Further evidence of low GQ is seen when men who do have good skills and knowledge are not willing to pass them on but keep them it to themselves out of fear that they will lose their own value or power if others know what they know. In the workplace, these men stop others from reaching their potential and hold them back because they feel threatened.

Our society needs young men with well developed forms of *all* types of intelligence: IQ, EQ, SQ and GQ. We need young men who have good mathematical and problem-solving skills but we also need young men who can form and sustain healthy relationships. Social Intelligence is vital so that they have awareness and understanding of how their actions affect society and the communities they live and work in. And we need young men with good Generational Intelligence who want to profit from the experience and the wisdom that older men and women have to offer. They will then add their own experience which they gain over time and will be keen to pass it on to the next generation of young men with good GQ.

The ability to find creative solutions to problems

We live in such a rapidly changing world with countless opportunities but also numerous potential issues and problems. Adaptability and being able to imaginatively come up with solutions is a vital life skill. How we live, what our relationships look like, the work we undertake and how we spend our spare time all require creative solutions. A one-dimensional focus where we believe that there is only one right way to do things or to live life puts a person at a distinct disadvantage.

One of the best ways to empower your son is to set him a challenge and encourage him to find a creative way of overcoming it. For example, if he is not doing well at school or struggling in a certain subject why not sit with him and together brainstorm what he could do about it. The conclusion may be that he could use a tutor, or he may have to organise his time better so that he can actually do the required study, or it may be that he would actually be better off not doing that subject at all. The key is to let him take the lead role in the discussion and for you to support him rather than telling him what he needs to do. (Which is much harder than it sounds for many of us!)

There's an old saying at Harvard University that a crisis is actually an opportunity, the belief being that when things go wrong it opens up new possibilities. Whenever things aren't working out for your son there is a chance to sit with him and say, 'Okay, what else could we be doing here? How could we turn this into a positive?'. Of course, a great way to teach is by example and creative problem solving is a worthwhile skill for all of us to practise.

Understanding the power of collaboration

Doing everything on your own is hard! Collaboration enables us to get so much more out of life. If your son has the ability and desire to work with other people then he will enjoy a far greater degree of support and success. In my organisation we want to run programs all over the country. Instead of trying to oversee everything ourselves we are much better off finding other organisations that already run similar programs and collaborating with them. If we combine our various resources we can achieve much more than we could alone.

I recently spent time talking with some young men who played in a band. Not only do they have to play their music together in such a way that all their individual instruments and voices combine to produce what they want – which in itself is a great example of collaboration – they also need to work together to make sure they are all available to attend practice, that they have a venue, as well as organising their various performances. What really impressed me was that one guy took charge of all the logistics of setting up, another organised the bookings, while another wrote the songs they played. It was extremely well organised and I could see that they were learning some great life skills while also having lots of fun doing what they loved.

Look for opportunities that will allow your son to practise collaborating. Building a skate board ramp with his mates, participating in activities through school, or playing team sports can be a great way to learn collaboration. As can being involved in groups like Scouts or The Foundation for Young Australians.

While the acquisition of life skills is essential in the development of a young man's psychology and critical in the maintenance of a healthy Personal Identity, his *physical* wellbeing is just as important. In the next chapter, we'll examine how vital it is to keep fit and active, no matter how old you are.

Key Points from Chapter 9

- Your son needs to learn certain key life skills as a young man

- He should understand the connection between privileges and responsibilities

- He needs to develop resilience if things don't go his way

- He should acquire good EQ, SQ and GQ

- He ought to be able to approach problems creatively

- He needs to appreciate the power of collaboration

CHAPTER 10

Physical health

It sounds obvious, but good physical health is vitally important if your son is to develop a healthy Personal Identity. It is much harder to get motivated, enjoy life and give things your all if you are unfit or overweight. Obviously, we can't alter our genes, but we can get healthy if we're willing to put in some effort. In order to be in top form, your son needs the following key things:

- Good healthy food
- Adequate sleep
- Regular exercise
- Time in nature.

Good healthy food

Young men can eat an enormous amount. My sons are always hungry and eat two to three times what I do. This is understandable. They are growing (fast) and their brains are going through a critical stage of development. It is important you give your sons the best and most healthy food possible, including lots of fresh fruit and vegetables.

It's also a good idea to avoid eating junk food, like fast food takeaways, soft drinks and lollies – anything with lots of sugar, fat and salt – however hard this may seem!

Sadly, a lot of young men live on junk food and other highly processed 'foods'. It is cheap and readily available but excess consumption will have disastrous effects on their health and wellbeing. The high sugar content in energy and other soft drinks or lollies, for example, spikes the glucose levels in their bloodstreams leading to a momentary increase in energy followed by a large release of insulin. This then leads to a dramatic drop in their circulating glucose and a 'crash' in energy levels. Takeaway food is often high in sugar as well as salt, unhealthy saturated fats and MSG (monosodium glutamate) – all of which have adverse health effects, especially on developing brains and bodies.

The best influence you can have on your son's eating habits is to eat well yourself. If you eat good healthy food then it is much easier to encourage your son to do the same. If you are always eating rubbish then your son will likely follow suit. If he has home-cooked meals with as much fresh local produce as possible and mini-mal processed and canned food, then his physical health – and in turn, his Personal Identity – will benefit. The other thing is not to have junk food in the house. If it's not there he can't eat it. You may not be able to control what he eats when he is out but he probably will still be having the majority of his meals at home. If he gets hungry and there are potato chips and chocolate in the cupboard that's what he will eat. If instead there is fresh fruit and vegetables around that are ready to eat 'fast foods' then he will eat those. (Boys aren't actually as picky eaters as you may think. It's more about quantity and the ability to keep eating so that they can deal with their almost constant hunger.)

Adequate sleep

Your son needs around 8.5 hours sleep *every* night. If he stays up too late watching TV, playing computer games or social networking, then he will be tired during the day and this will affect his ability to concentrate and learn. Tiredness can also cause irritability, lack of motivation, and in some cases contribute to depression.

Recent research shows that the explosion in interactive digital communication (emailing, texting and social networking) has meant that teenagers are getting on average two hours less sleep per night than they need. Even if they go to bed and turn off the light, they can still be under the covers tapping away on their smart phones. If you want your son to get the 8.5 hours sleep that he needs every night it may be necessary to insist that all phones and other devices are removed from his bedroom and stored elsewhere overnight. Even better, talk to him about it and make an agreement as to how much sleep he needs and what he needs to do in order to get it.

Regular exercise

No matter what age you are, regular exercise is critical for both physical and mental health. Exercise increases lung and heart capacity which increases blood flow and oxygen delivery throughout the body. Exercise builds muscle and makes us stronger. Exercise is just about the cheapest way to stave off illness, burn off excess energy, and correspondingly provide us with *extra* energy during the day. Exercise improves our appetite, gets rid of unnecessary fat and helps us sleep better. Exercise is fundamental and should be a integral part of *everybody's* daily routine – not just your teenage son's.

Time in nature

Nature Deficit Disorder, a term coined by the American author Richard Louv in his 2005 book *Last Child in the Woods*, refers to the modern trend of children spending less time outdoors. Louv says causes for this phenomenon include parental fears, restricted access to natural areas, and the irresistible lure of technology.

A generation of kids are growing up in concrete jungles, living mostly indoors. Instead of riding their bikes in the park after school they are spending hours and hours in their bedrooms playing computer games. Instead of playing sport or going camping on the weekend they are spending their spare time social networking or watching YouTube.

When I was at university (before computers and mobile phones) I thought that most of the kids who had grown up in the country and on farms were different somehow. They seemed genuine and practical and responsible types. They were easy-going and friendly with most everyone. My best mate's family lived on a cattle farm three hours out of the city and I used to go up there on weekends and holidays. In their kitchen they had a big wooden table with long benches either side and each night the whole family would gather round and eat together. There was always enough food and space for any guests that were passing through and laughter filled the house.

I used to get up early and split firewood before breakfast. I was not yet twenty years old and remember one morning using all my strength to try and break a really big log. To my horror I broke the handle of the axe instead. I thought I was done for. My mate's father came out of the house and took me and the broken axe to the shed. I was scared I was going to get in trouble but he didn't say anything for some time. Then he just set about making a new handle.

'You know, I never hit the wood as hard as I can,' he told me. 'That's when trouble can happen. Much better to concentrate more on hitting it in the *right* place, like where the cracks are. When I do that the wood splits a lot easier.' That old farmer gave me an invaluable life lesson that I have referred to many times since.

Get your sons outdoors, take them camping, spend

time with them in nature. Ask them to leave their electronic devices such as mobile phones and even watches behind. It may take them a while to unwind and slow down but when they do you will see a whole new side to their personalities. They'll quickly settle into their surroundings and become creative. In time, they'll start talking more and you'll enjoy discussions that simply can't occur when there are a million other things going on back at home. Nature will provide random life lessons which are invaluable. It's not a predictable and organised environment like the home often is. Young men have to think for themselves and they have to look after themselves. It's a very healthy, healing and enjoyable place for them to spend time.

• • •

Now that you've got an understanding of what your son is going through, what your new roles as parents or carers should be, and how best to equip your boy for the start of adult life, it's time to have a closer look at Rites of Passage (ROP), and how we can put a really effective modern-day version in place. Before we get into the practical aspects of Rites of Passage, I want to tell you a story from one of our early camps ...

Key Points from Chapter 10

- Physical health is vitally important for us all – but particularly for teenagers

- Healthy food, adequate sleep, plenty of exercise and time in nature are all needed

PART 3

RITES OF PASSAGE IN THE 21ST CENTURY

If we don't initiate our boys they will burn down the village in order to feel the heat.

African proverb

CHAPTER 11

A Rite of Passage story

It's late at night but deep in the bush it is anything but
silent. Crickets, frogs, owls and small marsupials create
a natural soundtrack. A group of boys makes their way
slowly along a bush track. They can't see very well in the
dark and the moon is only half-full, so they must rely on
the men who lead the way. They have been walking for
what seems like hours.

This has been one of the strangest days of their lives.
When they first arrived they had to hand in their mobile
phones, watches, portable gaming devices and any other
electronic equipment. These items were put in a big
metal box with a padlock for safe keeping. They spent
the rest of the day with their mums, chatting and laugh-
ing and hearing stories about when they were young.
Finally they had to say goodbye. Their mums told them
how much they loved them. Some of the mums cried as
they spoke. Finally, at dusk, a group of men arrived and
led the boys away …

The boys are now tired. They wonder where they are
going and how long they will have to keep walking. At
last, in the distance, they see flickering lights. As they

get closer they realise it's a fire. A group of men is waiting there for them. Some are their fathers, some their uncles, there is one grandfather, and there are a few men who are family friends who have agreed to come along as mentors. The boys notice there are also a few young men not much older than themselves whom they have not seen before; they look strong and are standing tall.

The men are happy to see them and greet them with handshakes and hugs. The boys stand close to their fathers or the man they came with but most don't talk and there is a sense of awkwardness. They don't really know each other and still aren't sure exactly what's going on. Some of them have never been away with their fathers before.

A hot dinner is served and it tastes delicious. After they eat it is time for bed and they wearily climb into their sleeping bags underneath a big shelter. Most are soon fast asleep. For some, however, it is a far from restful night. They are aware of the sounds of other men and boys nearby and the noises of the bush. Some have strange, unsettling dreams …

• • •

The following morning there's work to be done. Tents must be set up, firewood collected, breakfast prepared. All meals are eaten together around the camp fire. For the first time the boys get to properly check out everyone else on the camp. They are told the young men they saw last night are here to help out and will be working with the camp leaders. The boys have never experienced a group dynamic like this – they are used to football teams with one or two men coaching, or school classes with up to thirty kids and just a lone teacher (who is often a woman).

One boy separates from the others. He wears a hoodie. He hasn't said a word since he arrived.

After breakfast everyone sits in a big circle. Each boy has a man on either side of him. One of the camp leaders welcomes everyone and then explains that what is discussed in this and other 'talking circles' is both special and confidential. No one is allowed to go home and repeat what anyone else has said. He tells the group that the men are going to be asked to share stories about their lives. He reminds them that they are not allowed to tell the boys how to live their lives. They are not allowed to lecture them. They are not allowed to philosophise. They must only share their own personal stories.

The first story the men are asked to tell is about their own childhood, how it was for them when they were the age of the boy they have come with, and the relationship they had with their father.

Each man gets a chance to speak and while he does so he holds a stick. Only the man holding the stick speaks, no one interrupts or asks questions – this is his time. One by one the men share their stories and the boys watch and listen in silence and amazement. Quite a few men cry as they talk about their childhoods and their relationships with their dads. For most it was not an easy time and some had unsatisfactory or even bad relationships with their fathers. A couple didn't have dads at all and they speak about how hard that was.

After the men have finished it's the boys' turn to hold the stick. They are asked to talk about what sort of fathers they would like to be one day if they have children. This time the men listen in amazement as these boys who they have only just met and who are only just starting to grow fluff on their top lips speak with wisdom, positivity and insight. All the boys tell a story except for the one wearing the hoodie. He declines to speak, passes the stick along and sits fidgeting.

• • •

After the talking circle is over, games are played. The boys have energy to burn and they have push-up competitions then get a rope and organise a spontaneous tug-of-war against the men. The men win – but only just.

At lunchtime each boy eats with a man other than the one he has come with. The boys must find out what that man most enjoyed doing when he was a teenager and share with him the favourite things he likes to do. In-depth conversations are broken up by occasional bursts of laughter. After lunch there is a period of quiet time where each man and boy spend time alone with his thoughts. Some sleep in their tents, some sit under trees, and some lie back on the grass staring at the sky.

The camp fire is kept alight day and night. Only some of the men are allowed to put wood on the fire and only one man at a time looks after it. The boy with the hoodie spends a lot of his time near the fire.

One of the camp leaders notices and asks the boy if he'd like to look after the fire – to be the one to see that it has the right amount of wood and doesn't go out. The boy nods and there is a hint of a smile. He listens attentively as the man explains what to do. He even asks a few questions.

● ● ●

After just twenty-four hours together in the bush the group is already forming a strong bond. The boys are keen to help out and they do what they are asked. After dinner as the dishes are washed singing breaks out. The boy with the hoodie watches the fire like a hawk and keeps it just the right size, small in the day and bright and warm at night.

Each day follows a similar pattern. There are chores to be done and all must contribute; tasks are rotated so that everyone has a go in all areas. Each meal is varied and the boys get to eat with a different man and find out what they can about him. There are one or two talking circles every day. The topics are different, but the rules are always the same: only one person speaks at a time, and personal, true stories only are permitted. The men are asked to speak about:

- The relationship they had with their mothers when they were the boys' age and how it has changed
- Their experiences of grief and loss, including people they knew who have died
- How drugs and alcohol impacted their lives and the lives of people they know
- Their experiences of dating and their relationships with women
- Their greatest successes and their greatest failures.

At the end of each talking circle the boys are asked a question and given a chance to speak about:

- The relationship with their mothers and how they would they like them to evolve as they grow older
- Whether they have experienced grief and loss
- Whether drugs and alcohol are impacting on their lives and the lives of people they know
- Whether they are struggling with anything.

The bonding and trust within the group grow stronger with each session. Anybody who says that boys can't sit still and have poor attention spans is wrong. If the topic is interesting they'll sit and listen for hours!

The boys are allowed to ask questions at the end of each talking circle. After the discussion on dating and relationships one boy asks, 'What's the difference between having sex and making love?' The circle continues late into the evening.

• • •

At night everyone gathers around the camp fire. Some nights music is played, others feature lively discussions or sometimes no discussion at all. The men call it 'bush TV' and there is a special new show on every evening. The boy with the hoodie continues to tend the fire, though now he wears his hoodie pushed back off his face. Everyone is tired and goes to bed early.

One day is different. The boys are set a challenge: they must spend some time alone in the bush. While there, they are asked to think about what sort of men they want to be and what commitments they are ready to make about their future. They are also asked to think about what behaviours from their childhoods no longer work and need to be left behind.

This is a difficult experience for many of the boys: they're not used to being by themselves, let alone in the bush, and they don't know how long they will be there. They hear strange noises, insects and animals moving about, maybe even snakes. The camp leaders stay hidden watching the boys from a distance making sure that they are all okay.

When they return to camp there is a big celebration. They are no longer referred to by the others as boys, now they are called young men.

• • •

On the last full day of the camp everyone gathers in front of a big chair that has been decorated by the older men. One at a time the young men sit in the chair facing the group. The first young man has no idea what's going to happen. His father steps up and starts to speak. He tells his son what he loves about him, how special their relationship is and how much he loves spending time with him. The young man looks into his father's eyes and sees tears of love.

Then another man steps up and tells the young man what he has noticed about him while they've been on the camp. He tells him how he has admired certain qualities he has seen in him. A third man, one of the camp leaders, then gets up and also tells the young man the good qualities he has seen in him.

The young man can't believe his ears. No one has ever spoken to him like this before, no one has ever seen him in this way. He feels a bit shy and embarrassed but overwhelmingly proud and happy. He stands up and everyone starts shouting and cheering. He is welcomed into the group officially as a young man. He sits next to his dad feeling ten feet tall. His dad puts his arm around his shoulder and the young man shifts closer, comfortable in his embrace.

• • •

Finally it is time to leave, but before everyone packs up there are a few important things to do. The group walks to a nearby clearing. Two circles are formed with the young men on the inside and the older men on the outside. Each young man sits in front of an older man, though not the one he came to the camp with. The young man describes how he wants live his life, what his hopes and dreams are. They may not know exactly what they want to do with the rest of their lives but all have plenty to say. Then the older man tells the younger man what *he* wants to do. What his hopes and dreams are and how he wants to live. The young man with the hoodie no longer wears it at all – he is animated and engaged. After each pair has finished telling their stories they shuffle around the circle in order to speak with the next person in line.

This continues until eventually the young men sit facing their fathers, their uncles, grandfather or the man they came to the camp with. For the last time, they share their hopes and dreams and aspirations. Heads bend towards one another as intense conversations take place. Each listens with the same passion they have spoken with. It is another special moment.

• • •

After the group have returned to camp and eaten it is time to pack their gear and clean up the camp. Everyone works together and there is plenty of lively conversation and laughter. In a couple of hours everything is dismantled and has been loaded into a trailer ...

The group walk out of the camp along the bush track and finally out to the road. Eventually they see a hall in the distance with lots of cars parked outside. As they get nearer they see men and young boys waiting out the front. The welcoming party form a tunnel and those who have been on the camp pass through the tunnel to enter the hall. Young boys look enviously at their older brothers and the older men who have waited feel mixed emotions as they sense the strength and confidence of those returning.

The young men enter the hall and are momentarily taken aback. The hall is full of people – their mothers and other relatives and more friends – and has been decorated with flowers and brightly-coloured pieces of cloth. There is a huge table groaning with food and the young men smell the mouth-watering aromas wafting their way.

Circles are formed and the young men are publicly welcomed and celebrated. The young man who wore the hoodie stands tall and his mother has tears in her eyes as she proudly watches her son. At last the young men get to hug their mothers and those who have come to welcome them back. They feel strong and their mothers seem smaller. They feel lots of love. They notice some of the older men being warmly embraced by their partners. The food is served and the men eat with a newfound appreciation for the tastes and flavours of home.

It is time to leave. Most don't want to but it is getting late and the younger kids are tired. They get into their cars and immediately feel the strangeness of the modern world around them.

At home everything seems different. The men, young and old, reflect on their time at camp. Things people said, things they themselves said, things they witnessed. It is not easy being home and though they are tired and sleep deeply, they are also restless.

● ● ●

A camp reunion is held two weeks later and all the family is invited. It is wonderful to see everyone again. They sit in a big circle and each person shares something about what has been happening over the past couple of weeks. Then they separate and the men share what it has been like since the camp, what's been going well for them and if they have been struggling with anything. The women also sit in a circle and talk about what has been going on for them. Everyone has brought food and after the talking circles a meal is eaten. Small groups and pairs sit and eat together, most in deep conversation.

The men have decided they'd like to get together once a month. Next time they'll meet at the beach and go surfing; the following month a bushwalk is planned and in the school holidays they're thinking of going camping. One of the young men has set up a Facebook page for the group. Some of the older men aren't on Facebook but a couple of the young men volunteer to help them set up accounts.

Another camp has been arranged for later in the year. A new group of boys will have their time out in the bush. The young men are invited to come back and help out like the young men who were on their camp. The boy who wore the hoodie is the first to volunteer.

The camp has had a profound effect on everyone involved: lives have been changed forever; lifelong friendships made. Most importantly, the boys have publicly been recognised as becoming young men.

CHAPTER 12

Rites of Passage in the 21st century

I have been working with teenagers for thirty years and creating Rites of Passage (ROP) for young men for twenty. In this chapter I will explain the elements of a Rite of Passage and why each of them is so important.

The words 'Rite of Passage' mean different things to different people. I have spoken to both men and women who don't like the idea at all because it reminds them of a time in their lives when something bad (or just plain weird) happened.

> Ron is sixty-two and remembers when he started university. 'All the first year students were told they had to come to the hall at 6 pm. When we got there, we were taken inside by older students wearing masks. The windows had been blacked out. We were forced to strip to our underpants and blindfolds were put over our eyes. We sat on the cold floor for ages until one at a time we were picked up and the blindfolds were taken off. For nearly two hours we underwent all sorts of humiliating acts. We

had to eat disgusting things like raw liver and eggs. In between we had to drink whole cans of beer and all the while the older students were standing around us with horse whips hitting us around the legs if we stopped or tried to resist. Some of the students vomited and a few were even crying.

'At one stage, they had a huge block of ice with a hole in the middle and they pulled down my underpants and made me pretend to have sex with it. All the older students from the university were sitting around watching and they cheered and hollered while this was happening.

'Finally it was over and we were given back our clothes. The older students lined up as a tunnel and as we left the hall they clapped and shook our hands. There was a big party afterwards and most people went but I didn't. I felt sick and just wanted to be alone. What I am most ashamed of though is that the next year when the new students came I was one of those in the hall forcing them to go through exactly the same ritual.'

What Ron experienced in the story above is indeed a type of Rite of Passage (ROP). But it is a type of inappropriate, unsupervised ROP, an example of all the things *not* to do. It is a classic case of what happens when society doesn't create proper and respectful ROP for its young men: they go and do it themselves!

When I was eighteen and studying in Jerusalem, I lived with a group of guys from South America. They told me that when they had turned thirteen they all went down to the local brothel and had their first sexual experience. In most cases it was their dads who gave them the money! They went as a group and they all lost their virginity on the same day, many of them with the same woman. Afterwards they were considered to be men. This was their version of a Rite of Passage.

Gangs sometimes require new members to steal something, or even get into a fight so that they can prove they are man enough to be admitted to the gang. Boys are attracted to this – especially if they see there is little else in society that can make them feel like and be seen as a man.

These cases demonstrate what happens when society stops creating healthy and appropriate Rites of Passage (ROP). Young men go DIY: often with disastrous, life-long consequences. Our boys are all going to become men at some stage and they need a ROP in order to do so. As parents and as a society we have a choice: either we create a healthy and respectful community-based ROP, or we leave boys to create their own.

A Rite of Passage should *never* be a negative, embarrassing, humiliating or dangerous experience. It should be cause for celebration because it is marking the growth and change of the boy into a young man – someone we want to be happy and successful.

Here are four important things to remember:

- We already have many existing Rites of Passage that we consider normal in modern society
- Rites of Passage (ROP) have always been important to indigenous societies and cultures and they all had a Boy-to-Man ROP
- A Boy-to-Man ROP is the missing link that can create *exactly* the transition we need for our boys to become healthy and successful young men
- We have the ability and responsibility to create many different types of appropriate, modern-day Boy-to-Man ROP.

What exactly is a Rite of Passage?

As I have mentioned, Rites of Passage (ROP) are not new, and we already have many as part of our everyday lives. Anything that marks the transition from one stage in life to another is a Rite of Passage.

I remember clearly the day I graduated as a doctor. All the students had to get dressed up in cloaks and hats. The heads of the university were also dressed up and after lots of speeches we ascended the stage one at a time to receive our certificates. My family and friends were there, as were hundreds of other families and their friends. After that day I became Dr Rubinstein and I was no longer a student. Now I could practise medicine, I could treat people and I could be paid for my services. Life would never be the same and the moment had been marked.

My graduation was a Rite of Passage, as are weddings, birthday parties, and retirement dinners. A Rite of Passage is simply a way of marking the fact that life and your role in it will now be permanently different. It is a way for you to understand this but as importantly it is also a way for society to acknowledge it too.

An event to mark a change in a person's life

The words *'Rites de Passage'* were first coined by the nineteenth-century French anthropologist Arnold van Gennep who studied indigenous communities around the world. Van Gennep found that all traditional societies had a 'ritual way of creating a passageway to pass from one stage in life to the next'.

Think about two stages in life as though they are two rooms with a passageway in between. In the first room, to continue my earlier example, I am a student. I walk along the passageway, and when I reach the second room I am a doctor. The passageway between the two rooms is where the Rite of Passage occurs. Without the passageway it can be difficult or messy getting from one room to the other, and thus from one stage in life to the next. I may find myself in the second room but still feel like I am in the first. Or I may feel like I am in the first room but believe that I should be in the second! Nothing has clearly marked or signalled the transition.

Paul was seventeen when he left school and went to work in a factory. 'All of a sudden I'd gone from playing in the schoolyard to working with men, tough men with big arms and deep voices. I was supposed to do the same work as them and I tried everything I could to be like them but I still felt like such a boy and it was really uncomfortable. It was even worse when I went home because it was there that I didn't feel like a boy any more. I had money in my pocket and I'd been working and swearing all day but my mum still treated me like a child. It made me angry and I said some horrible things to her. I know it wasn't her fault but it was all just so confusing and I didn't know who I was any more or how I was supposed to be.'

A ritual (a custom or ceremony)

A ritual marks the Rite of Passage as something that is special and is conducted with respect. A ritual also suggests that it is a practice that has been done many times before, and that it will be repeated in the future. The actions which take place in a ritual are typically traditional to the community, have high symbolic, value and have been handed down over generations. In the West, graduations and weddings have been a part of our lives for hundreds of years. At these times, we wear special clothes that we would never otherwise wear, and we often say particular verses to bless the occasion, or make speeches. These are all traditions which give the Rite of Passage gravitas, which make it serious. They also make the Rite of Passage real and to many people even sacred. I was keenly aware at my graduation that thousands of medical students before me had gone through the same Rite of Passage when they became doctors.

Rituals are also usually witnessed by a community so everyone knows that the person going through the Rite of Passage is now entering a new life stage and acquiring a new status. That's why my family and friends came to my graduation, and that's why weddings traditionally have lots of guests.

The Boy-to-Man Rite of Passage

Of all the Rites of Passage (ROP) that indigenous societies conducted, the one that was given the most attention, the one that they all did, and the one that they considered the most important, was the Boy-to-Man ROP. Sadly, while so many other ROP still exist in the West, the Boy-to-Man ROP is the one that we have lost from our traditions.

Why we need a modern Boy-to-Man Rite of Passage

If our young men were going well, if our leaders were looking after our world in a fair and sustainable way, and if relationships were thriving, then it would be reasonable to say we didn't need a Boy-to-Man Rite of Passage. However, the evidence overwhelmingly proves that our teenage sons are in crisis, the leadership of men is harming our planet, and relationships are falling apart like at no other time in history.

Indigenous tribes and communities stretching back thousands of years put enormous effort into their Rites of Passage. They realised that the fundamental shift from boy psychology to healthy man psychology had to occur *at the same time* as the physical transformation. For these societies, this shift was far too important to be left up to the random processes and trials of life. Without a Boy-to-Man Rite of Passage the tribe risked over-grown boys rather than healthy, capable men taking control.

This was of practical concern, but it was also a matter of survival: these tribes needed full participation from *all* its members; there was simply no room for self-indulgent, destructive or boyish behaviour. Their future depended on having true leaders – real men who saw their lives and responsibilities differently from how a boy sees them. These societies needed men who would look after the other members of the tribe. They needed men who would protect their resources so there would be food and shelter available for the future.

Arnold van Gennep found that no matter where in the world, traditional societies created Boy-to-Man Rites of Passage that had the same three basic phases of 'separation', 'transition' and 'return'.

1) The separation
- The first stage was when the boys were taken away by the male elders and separated from the rest of the community.

2) The transition
This was when the actual change took place and always involved the following:
- The history, values, beliefs and knowledge of the community would be passed on to the boy
- A challenge that involved overcoming fears and difficulties was created
- The elders would recognise and acknowledge the young man's individual gifts.

3) The return

- The final stage was when the men returned and the whole community would gather to witness and celebrate the completed transition.

Rites of Passage today

In modern society, it is of course no longer appropriate to conduct an indigenous-style Rite of Passage – especially when we consider some of the things that used to happen. In Africa, boys had to hunt and kill a lion or other wild animal with a spear; in Vanuatu they jumped head-first off a high bamboo tower with a vine tied around their ankle that barely stopped them from hitting the ground. Boys of the Algonquin Indians of Quebec were brought to a secluded area, caged, and then given an intoxicating medicine known as *wysoccan*, an extremely dangerous hallucinogen one hundred times more powerful than LSD. The Amazonian Satere Mawe tribe performed Rites of Passage whereby their young men had to place their hands inside mittens filled with hundreds of bullet ants and leave them there for a period of time. The bite is twenty times more painful than a wasp sting and the pain can last up to twenty-four hours! At the end of a Rite of Passage in some Australian Aboriginal communities (and in the African Maasai), boys were circumcised; while in other communities one of their front teeth was knocked out. In New Zealand and Tahiti boys were tattooed.

The length of time dedicated to a traditional Rite of Passage could be weeks or months and even longer. In the Sambia tribe in Papua New Guinea, boys spent up to ten years away from their mothers!

These traditions may sound horrific, cruel, dangerous and irresponsible. However, let's look at what is happening today when we don't create a Rite of Passage for our boys. These days young men don't go out and face lions with spears or jump off towers with vines around their ankles, but they do other equally dangerous things, like speeding, getting into fights, getting drunk, train surfing or base jumping. Too many young men are dying through such extreme risk-taking behaviour.

We do not give our young men ceremonial drugs to help them gain deeper insights and yet the availability and use of illegal drugs is something all our boys will be exposed to at some time, and drug addiction is a major issue for young people. We don't circumcise, knock out teeth or ritually tattoo young men, yet increasing numbers are getting piercings and tattooing themselves all over their bodies. We don't take our boys away from their mothers for lengthy periods so they can grow up and be independent, but sadly many young men end up shutting down from their mums and pushing them away for years.

In effect, boys are creating their own Rites of Passage (ROP) and they are doing so unfacilitated and unsupported. Gangs, fraternities, clubs, teams and any institutions that involve rituals all practise forms of ROP, but unfacilitated and unsupervised ROP are usually inappropriate, damaging for your boy's wellbeing and frequently dangerous. They may well include the three key principles of story, challenge and recognition of a young man's gifts. However, instead of the story of his community, the young man might learn the folklore of the gang or club. There is a risk that he will be asked to do something stupid or dangerous in order to be accepted into the group. Belonging may be so important that he may risk his life or the possibility of going to jail.

It is unlikely he will be recognised for his true gifts but rather for something that relates to the values of that particular group. A gang might honour a young man for being a good fighter; a bunch of mates might honour each other for being able to drink the most or for misbehaving at school.

This is not healthy behaviour and we risk ending up with men who believe their sporting team is more important than their family, who want to relive old glories or who as grown men look for every opportunity to get together with their mates and do stupid things.

After all my years working with young people I am convinced we *can and need* to bring the essence of the traditional Rite of Passage that has been developed over countless generations into an appropriate modern-day setting. I am also positive that by doing so we will prevent many young men trying to initiate themselves into manhood – with all the disastrous side-effects that go along with that.

The three phases of separation, transition and return are as relevant now as they have ever been. If done properly they will directly and positively impact a young man's healthy Personal Identity. A modern-day Rite of Passage will help a young man have:

1. Healthy family relationships
2. Key life skills
3. Good physical and mental health
4. Recognition of and encouragement to pursue his unique gifts and talents
5. Support through the critical transition period from boy to young man.

As you will have read in the previous chapters, in the 1990s, I helped develop a program that created a modern-day Rite of Passage. We took groups of boys between the ages of thirteen and fifteen camping in the bush. All the boys were accompanied by a man. Many came with their dads, others came with a relative or mentor. They had to leave their watches, electronics, mobile phones and any reading material behind. During the week we shared stories, created challenges and honoured each of the young men. We also laughed a lot, played music, sang songs and ate great food. At the end the camp we had a celebration with all the mothers as well as friends and relatives.

We were astounded by the power and the effect of these programs. Something special and life-changing happened for both the boys *and* their fathers or mentors. I have kept in contact with many of those who have attended our programs and have collected feedback via hundreds of quotes and testimonials. Here are some of my favourites:

'It was the best week of my life.' **Sam, aged fourteen**

'I am a single mother and my son and I had been fighting a lot. I didn't know what to do. Since he has come back he has totally changed. Now we talk and he is happy to help around the house. I don't know what you men did out there but it worked.' **Helena, aged thirty-seven**

'A man should be able to show his emotions and be a warrior and show his soft side and be a real gentleman. And to be around all that, it showed me that it really is out there.' **Christo, aged fifteen**

'My dad honouring me was the best thing that has happened to me in my whole life.' **Peter, aged sixteen**

'The challenge was the hardest thing I have ever done but it's really helped me so much. I used to always give up when things weren't easy. Now I can look back on it and know when things get tough that I can make it through. All I have to do is believe in myself.'
Brett, aged nineteen

'I learned so much just from listening to the men tell their stories. I had no idea they struggled when they were my age with so many of the things that I struggle with. I thought it was just me. If they can get through it then I know that I can.'
Josh, aged seventeen

'Even though it's nearly ten years since my son and I went on the program it has changed our relationship forever and we still refer back to it. We now have a way of being able to relate to each other as men.'
James, aged fifty-six

'I think about other people more now than I used to. I wasn't mean, but I just didn't consider how other people felt … Now I think about that more. That happens when you're grown up, when stuff is wrong you notice a lot more and try to do something about it.'
Dean, aged sixteen

The impact of a 21st-century Boy-to-Man Rite of Passage

A 21st-century Boy-to-Man Rite of Passage (ROP) positively contributes to *all* five elements on a young man's PI scale. Let's look at them one by one.

Healthy family relationships

When a boy hears his father's stories he sees him in a whole new light. He realises that his father is human and just like him there are things he has struggled with and overcome. He realises that his father has wisdom borne from experience. When a boy is honoured and recognised for his gifts and talents, a shift can occur in the father/son relationship. The son knows that he is now being seen by his father as a young man in his own right. The relationship changes from the boy being told by his father what to do into one where as two individuals they can work together. Dad can genuinely support his son, who one day will hopefully do the same in return.

When a boy has time to reflect on what his mother has done for him, to think about how she has cared for him since he was a baby and to hear other men and boys talking about their mothers, he gains a newfound appreciation and love for her as a woman. This will form the basis of a deeply respectful relationship not only for her but for all the women in his life.

When a mother acknowledges that her son is becoming a young man and that she has to let him go to live his own life then a new relationship based on respect and healthy communication can be formed. This can be the start of a lifelong loving and close relationship where she no longer has to mother her son but can enjoy supporting him in a different way as he becomes a man. At the same time, she is also free to pursue her own passions in life.

Key life skills (EQ, SQ and GQ, connecting privileges with responsibility, resilience, collaboration)

The stories the boys hear during a Rite of Passage work on all levels of their intelligence. Emotional Intelligence is improved when they see and experience first-hand how older men feel. There are no distractions when someone speaks, no mobile phones or computers. Everyone is present and paying attention and it's near impossible not to feel the emotions behind what a man is saying.

Social Intelligence benefits from hearing not only the stories but the impact that the experiences the men describe have had on them and on others. If a man shares that his marriage fell apart as a result of years of devoting his life to work (or booze or other distractions) and not being there for his family, his son will realise that his actions have an impact beyond his own life.

Generational Intelligence is acquired because the boys are learning from those who came before them – not by being told what to do, but by listening and absorbing. There is a greater chance they will be wiser and won't make the same mistakes in their own lives.

Connecting privileges with responsibility is demonstrated through the stories as the boys listen to the men sharing their life experiences. The boys understand early on that it is actually a privilege to be hearing these deep and often very private stories. In return, they have a responsibility to be respectful at all times and to agree to maintain confidentiality so that each of them can feel safe to share their truth.

Resilience is also demonstrated through the stories as the men speak of difficult times, grief and loss but also how they were able to continue on with their lives despite the hardships.

Finally, collaboration is a pivotal part of the program as everyone on the camp works together and has different roles in order to create a community in the bush that can feed and support them for their time away.

Good physical health
Good healthy food, regular exercise and adequate sleep are all vital parts of a camp. Ideally the camps are also run in beautiful outdoor locations to take advantage of the extra magic created by being in nature and breathing fresh air. The boys also meet and observe older men who have looked after themselves and lived healthy lives.

Recognition of and encouragement to pursue his unique gifts and talents
The honouring of the young man by his father or mentor as well as other men in front of his peers and men that

he respects is direct recognition of his unique gifts and talents. The boy will be encouraged to pursue what is best for both him and his community. This goes a long way in bolstering the health of young man's Personal Identity and has tremendous long-term impact.

Traditional societies believe that each individual has a unique spirit inside them and that this spirit defines not only who that person is but also their place in the community. Spirits aren't always immediately obvious but have to be discovered and then recognised publicly.

A boy's 'spirit being' would be announced and revealed to him during his Rite of Passage. At this time he would also receive a new name. This act served to give the young man his place in the community. A boy may be seen as having the spirit of the firemaker, another may possess the spirit of the storyteller, or the hunter. Through knowing their spirit being they could then connect with their life's true purpose and role. The person with the spirit of the fire would be in charge of the fires that provided warmth at night. The person with the spirit of the storyteller would hold the community's history and would then be responsible for passing it on to future generations, the hunter would provide food, and so forth.

Modern, Western society has taught us a much more scientific approach to finding your life's purpose. However, it is recognised within academic circles that different people are good at different things. Some are naturally skilled mathematically, some musically while some excel at sport. It is also widely acknowledged that if someone has a natural talent and is given the opportunity and encouragement to pursue that talent they are more likely to succeed. It therefore stands to reason that if we want our sons to reach their maximum potential we need to identify what they are naturally good at and encourage them to pursue it. Whether you say we are naming the spirit of the young man or whether you say we are recognising and celebrating his strengths – it doesn't really matter. More often than not they are effectively the same thing.

This acknowledgement and honouring will not only help our boys on a personal level but it will also mean we will end up with men who are motivated to work hard at what they are good at and what they love doing. This is so different from the lives of so many men who spend their careers doing something they really don't enjoy.

Support through the critical transition from boy to young man

The aim of creating a 21st-century Boy-to-Man Rite of Passage (ROP) is to acknowledge that the transition *needs* a ROP in order to properly and fully happen. The support comes by providing the ROP in a safe, appropriate, community-based way with facilitators who understand the process they are undertaking.

The boys have a life-changing experience and importantly they learn that in the future they will have people they can speak to and who will support them to live their lives to the fullest, who will help them continue to seek their true purpose, and who will be there in their times of need.

The shift from boy psychology to healthy man psychology

After young men return from the Rite of Passage they won't miraculously be fully-fledged adults who suddenly know everything and have got it all together. They certainly will have changed but it's more realistic if we think of them almost as 'baby men'. They are no longer boys and are now ready to take their first steps in this exciting new stage of life.

The Rite of Passage will have planted a seed. Over time this seed will grow and as a result in the future these young men will be better fathers, better husbands and partners, and better community members. They still have a lot of learning to do, they will still stumble and no doubt make mistakes, but if they are supported and nurtured in the right way, they will slowly but surely grow into men with healthy Personal Identities who live in healthy man psychology.

Good mentors

There is another important outcome of a properly run Boy-to-Man Rite of Passage. All the men present will know by the end that they are not there only for the young man that they came with for *all* of the young men. They will realise that if the young man they came with has a problem and feels he needs someone other than his father to talk to there will be other men he can approach. The young man will know that he has any number of men he can now talk to and safely spend time with. This is a powerful new support system.

The young man will also know that he is not alone and men in the community are watching him and are interested in what he is doing. They want him to be happy and successful but they will also know if he gets in trouble or behaves inappropriately. He will feel drawn to his passion and guided by the knowledge of his gifts and talents that have been publicly named and honoured. He will also know that he has a responsibility to all present, to his family, to his friends and to his community.

What about boys without fathers?

I met Nick when he was thirteen. He lived with his grandmother. She heard me speaking on the radio and rang to see if he could come to a camp. She told me that Nick had been getting in trouble at school and was in danger of being expelled. We arranged a meeting and had a long talk. Nick wouldn't look directly at me and didn't talk much, however when I asked him what he loved doing he opened up bit and talked about his favourite music. I got a glimpse of another side of him which was sparky and fun. Nick had never been camping but he said he would like to come on our program so I offered him a scholarship and we found a mentor to come with him.

Nick was shy and wary when he arrived at the camp and said very little. After a couple of days when he did eventually speak in one of the circles it was profound. He told us about the tragedy of his family situation, what he had been through and why it was that he had to live with his grandmother. He also told us that he really wanted to learn the guitar. We had a couple of guitarists on the camp and they gave Nick his first lessons. I watched him spend as much time as he could practising and sitting talking to the other men and boys. One of the men took it upon himself to arrange some lessons for Nick after the camp and gave him an old guitar to use. The mentor who brought Nick on the camp kept in contact with him and Nick also spent time staying with some of the other young men he had made friends with.

Exactly one year later, Nick returned to another camp, this time not as a boy but as a young man who would help out and be part of the leadership team. His grandmother dropped him off and I watched as he went straight to the boot of the car and pulled out a guitar case with what was obviously his prized possession inside. For the duration of the camp Nick delighted us with soulful tunes and songs, some of which he had written himself. He was open and friendly with a smile from ear to ear. While the men were impressed, the younger boys thought he was a legend.

On some of the Rites of Passage camps we have run, over half the boys are brought by men who are not their fathers. This is a sad insight into the extent of the breakdown in families. But on a positive note, it is a great sign that there are men in the community who are prepared to step up and support boys whose fathers are not present. While of course it would be great if every boy could come on a program with his dad, the reality is that it simply is not always going to happen. That does not mean we cannot create a meaningful Rite of Passage for these boys. I have seen countless boys without fathers benefit enormously from attending with a mentor. I hope that more men will become involved in this work so that all boys can attend programs and be supported on their journey.

Now that we have an understanding of why a properly run and facilitated Boy-to-Man Rite of Passage (ROP) is necessary – and what can happen when parents and carers *don't* get involved – let's look at how we can make successful Rites of Passage a reality.

Key Points from Chapter 12

- We have many Rites of Passage that already exist in our everyday lives

- A Rite of Passage marks a significant change in a person's life

- If we don't create a Rite of Passage for our boys they will create their own with potentially disastrous consequences

- There are always the same key elements in a Rite of Passage - separation, transition and return

- A Boy-to-Man Rite of Passage positively helps all five areas on a young man's PI scale

CHAPTER 13

How to get involved in a 21st-century Boy-to-Man Rite of Passage

There are two ways of getting your son involved in a 21st-century Boy-to-Man Rite of Passage (ROP) – you can join an established program run by a professional organisation, or you can create and implement your own Rite of Passage with the help of friends and family. Both options can work.

In traditional Rites of Passage there were always specific people in the community whose role it was to take charge. Today, there are growing numbers of organisations and people being trained in Rites of Passage who understand their importance and are running excellent programs. This is happening all over the world. At the back of this book is a list of contact details for a number of reputable organisations. I highly recommend you consider this as you will be dealing with people who have committed to creating the best programs possible based on years of research and experience.

If you cannot find a suitable organised program near you then you have the option of creating your own. If you decide to do this, you must include the three key stages of separation, transition and return. And within the transition stage, there must be story, challenge and honouring. Also there must be an appropriate follow-up after the Rite of Passage, and I will explain later in this chapter how to do that.

Ideally, a 21st-century Boy-to-Man Rite of Passage (ROP) will be accomplished in a single event over a fixed period of time. This is a great option as it allows everyone to really focus on what is happening and to make sure that all the elements of the ROP are properly covered and flow into each other in the best way possible.

If necessary, the Rite of Passage can be accomplished over a longer period, as time and commitments allow: for example, over the course of a school year. This will create some challenges but if you understand what you are doing and what is happening then with the right help you will be able to do it successfully.

Whichever option you choose, to create a successful Boy-to-Man Rite of Passage for your son you must do the following five things:

1. Get the timing right
2. Research, plan and understand the process as best you can
3. Enlist the help of others
4. Make sure *all* the elements are covered properly
5. Be respectful and safe.

Get the timing right

Firstly the right time will not be the same for every boy. Some have physically changed and are emotionally ready by the age of twelve; others develop later and will not be ready until they are fourteen, fifteen or even sixteen. Generally, the majority of boys are ready between the ages of thirteen or fourteen but in the nearly twenty years that I have been running programs I have seen the age decrease by around twelve months and more often, twelve-year-olds are ready. I put that down to the internet and the exposure to all sorts of material that simply was not available to young boys twenty or even ten years ago.

Aside from the physical changes, the timing will be right when you notice your son starting to change in other ways ... and believe me, you *will* notice. It might be the way he talks to you, or his general change in attitude. He may get in trouble at school or start locking the door to his bedroom or the bathroom. He may not want to spend as much time with you, or he may suddenly become short tempered. These are all signs that he is ready.

If he is too young he will struggle with the psychological shifts required. If you wait too long and he already has a couple of years in the difficult in-between time, he may resist and it will be harder work. It is not too late though and a Rite of Passage *is* possible at the age of sixteen or seventeen – or even older. You still incorporate the principles of story, challenge and honouring.

However, it will be different for an older boy and you will need to use your commonsense and seek help to ensure you get the process right.

> Malidoma Some came from the Dagara Tribe in Burkina Fasa in Africa. As a four-year-old boy he was taken away by white men and grew up in a mission. He missed the time when the other boys in his tribe were going through their Rite of Passage. Many years later as a twenty-year-old Malidoma ran away and somehow found his way back to his village. Despite being much older than the other boys, after he was accepted back into the tribe, he was put through their Boy-to-Man Rite of Passage. The villagers knew that they could not have a boy in a man's body living among them.

In traditional societies a boy's parents were considered too close to him to be able to decide the timing of his Rite of Passage. Understandably, they were also often reluctant to let their boy go and would try to hold onto him for as long as possible. The boy's grandparents were usually the ones who determined when he was ready. Grandparents were close enough to be able to see clearly but old and wise enough to know when the timing was right.

Research, plan and understand the process as best you can

The second thing you need to do is learn as much as you can about what a Rite of Passage is and what each of the three stages – story, challenge and honouring – involve. Hopefully the preceding chapter will have laid the foundations but at the end of this book you'll also find a list of recommended further reading. Please also refer to my website for additional information.

Enlist the help of others

It is vital you don't attempt to create and conduct a Rite of Passage (ROP) all on your own. Historically, it was never the parents who ran their own boy's ROP. Aim to enlist as many people as possible who have been involved in your son's life, especially those who you respect and whose stories you would like your son to hear. Explain to them what a ROP is and what you are trying to achieve. Chances are they'll be supportive and will work out for themselves their role in the process. In fact, you'll be surprised at the effort, enthusiasm and creativity your friends and family will invest. Even just knowing that your son is going through a ROP and being there at the end to acknowledge him as a young man will be seen as an important privilege to be included in.

It's also worthwhile looking for people in your community who have an existing involvement in Rite of Passage work. A growing number of people understand the importance of ROP and are undertaking training in the field. Many will be willing to help – me included – so please get in touch if you need to.

If you are a single parent, try as best you can to involve the other parent. Remember that this process is not about your relationship with that person, it is about your son's relationship with them. I've witnessed many occasions where mums would tell me that their son's father was not around, that he hadn't been involved in their son's life until now and that there was no way he was going camping! I would say to those mothers that even if the father has not played an active part in the son's life so far, that doesn't mean it has to continue that way in the future. The Rite of Passage can be the turning point.

In my experience, most kids when given a choice want a relationship with *both* their parents. A Rite of Passage can be the perfect opportunity for this to happen. Often, I would find myself on the phone to a mother or father who was supposedly not interested in being involved only to discover that when it was explained they were then very keen to be a part of this important process.

Make sure **all** the elements are covered properly

The three key stages of separation, transition and return must *all* be included for the Rite of Passage to work. Separation has to occur so that your son understands that his time as a boy has come to an end. Within transition, he then has to hear the stories of men, face a challenge and be honoured and acknowledged for his unique gifts and talents. The return is just as important as it allows the public recognition by family, friends and community of the fact that your boy is now a young man. If the return stage is not included in the Rite of Passage then the young man may still be seen and treated like a boy – despite what he has gone through. This can be confusing and wounding for him and can force him to retreat back into an unhealthy in-between place.

Be respectful and safe

I cannot emphasise this enough. A Rite of Passage (ROP) is a huge responsibility and the welfare of your son is of the utmost importance. A true ROP has nothing to do with the school yard-style 'initiations' of beatings or toilet baptisms you occasionally hear about or see on TV. There is nothing violent or sadistic about a properly run Boy-to-Man Rite of Passage. It should be conducted with the greatest respect and honouring of the young man. After all, the purpose is to bring him into manhood – not to break or damage him.

Safety is so important and is always a concern when you're in an unfamiliar environment like the bush, and particularly when you are setting challenges. Be sure to involve people you trust and respect. Carefully plan what you intend to do and discuss it with them to make sure that your ideas are sensible and well thought through. Always devise a safety plan in case something goes wrong.

The more planning, care and effort that is put into

the Rite of Passage, the more everyone will get out of it. Treat this as one of the most important things you will ever do in your life. It is.

Key Points from Chapter 13

- You can do a Boy-to-Man Rite of Passage through an established organisation – or create your own

- Get the timing right, understand the process, enlist help, make sure all elements are covered and be safe

CHAPTER 14

Creating your own Boy-to-Man Rite of Passage

Once you have decided on the timing, learned all you can about the key elements of a Rite of Passage (ROP), and enlisted the help of others, it is finally time to make it happen. Because you are creating your own version, there are unlimited ways to go as long as you follow the general principles. Below I give some guidelines and suggestions, but the exact shape and duration of the ROP is now up to you and those who are helping you.

The separation

During this stage, your boy needs to go somewhere that is different to where he normally lives. There needs to be older men involved in the Rite of Passage and that may or may not include the boy's father. The group, small or large, could go camping or fishing, go somewhere overseas, or visit a friend or relative's holiday house. You may only be able to go for a weekend; if it is school holidays you may be able to take a week or even more. The longer the better. Having more time means that the process can run deeper. All too often we are trying to do important things in life in the shortest time possible. This can reduce the impact. In traditional societies a Boy-to-Man ROP could take weeks, months or even years! These cultures realised they had an awful lot to accomplish and impart during this process.

Mums (along with sisters, aunties and other female relatives and friends) do *not* go on a Rite of Passage. This is a time when a boy must separate from his mum so that he can go away, transition, and then return to create a new relationship with her. Mums and their sons should spend plenty of time together *before* he leaves. In the lead-up to a Rite of Passage, mums should tell their sons they can see he is approaching adulthood and that soon he will be a young man. Prepare yourself for his reaction: he may think you have gone a little crazy and he may well even resist. Lots of boys are in no hurry to grow up as there are many advantages in acting and being treated like a child. Spend time talking about his childhood. Boys love hearing stories of when they were little – what they got up to and what they were like. Tell him about when he was born, what sort of a baby he was, when he first walked or talked, what his favourite foods were, what he enjoyed doing, what he got in trouble for, and so on. While you're at it, tell him about when *you* were a kid and how it was for you growing up … and be ready to answer questions as there may be plenty!

Separation marks the end of a boy's dependence on his mum. A unique part of the mother/son relationship is coming to an end. It doesn't mean that from now on your son will be totally independent and have nothing to do with you, but things are going to change. You might find this challenging and may not like the idea of your baby no longer needing you. Understand though that they *do* still need you – only in a different way. For their own good, you have to be able to let them go so that they can grow into healthy, balanced men. Allow yourself to explore your own feelings. Talk about these feelings with those closest to you and give yourself some time and space.

> Anna reflects on when her son did his Rite of Passage. 'He was my first-born son and I was amazed at my grief when he left. My baby was growing up. I cried for days and couldn't stop thinking about him as a young child. The thought that he would never be my little baby again felt like a part of me had died.'

If time is an issue

For some families it just won't be possible to spend a week or even a weekend creating a Boy-to-Man Rite of Passage. However, as I have said, it is still possible to implement the three key elements of separation, transition and return over a longer period. You will just have to be a bit more inventive. Please get advice as you can't do it on your own.

The transition
This central part of a Rite of Passage contains three elements: story, challenge, and recognising his unique gifts and talents.

Story
In a traditional Rite of Passage a boy would learn the history of his people. In some tribes the story was told through dance, in others through song, in others through art. Some tribes had designated storytellers who would recount the myths and legends of the community. The boy was told and shown things that he would not have seen or known previously. In cultures without books, telling stories was the only way for history to pass on knowledge from one generation to the next.

A boy would also be shown and introduced to the world of men. This might involve being taught about hunting animals, learning about women, how to survive in the desert or forest, the use of weapons, and the spiritual beliefs of the tribe.

Recounting stories about particular people and events is a far better way of illustrating life lessons to a young man than telling him what to do. For thousands of years, humans have sat around fires sharing stories and passing on the history of their communities. This tradition is as valuable today as it always has been.

Here are some tips about storytelling that we have found work really well when incorporated into a ROP:

1. Only one person talks at a time.

No one may interrupt or ask questions while a man is speaking. Give the man speaking an object to hold, for example a stick or a ball. Until he puts the object down, he has the space and freedom to talk.

2. Only personal stories may be told. Lecturing and philosophising are *not* allowed.

Teenagers are not interested in being *told* how to live their lives. They will shut down if you lecture them, even though they may be looking straight at you and appearing to listen! On the other hand they love hearing real stories of men's experiences and how those experiences affected them and shaped their lives.

3. Confidentiality, confidentiality, confidentiality.

Everyone must agree at the start that whatever is said in the 'talking circles' during a Rite of Passage is confidential and will not be repeated afterwards. The reason for this is that we are asking men to share stories about the most significant times in their lives, and the most important things that ever happened to them. Only if a man knows that he can do so in complete safety – which must include total confidentiality – will he feel comfortable speaking openly.

4. Create a storytelling space.

If you can, create a special space for the storytelling. If everyone comes into that space respectfully, listens to the stories and then leaves, it will be even more powerful. Make sure there are no interruptions like phones ringing or people randomly coming or going. It may be that you put all the chairs or couches in a circle or you sit around a table, or a camp fire. It is a good idea if everyone can clearly see everyone else in the group.

At the end of each storytelling session give the boys a chance to ask questions. Once again, the answers should come in the form of a clarification of the events or another story rather than dictating to the boys how to live their lives.

Your son can't learn everything from you, he needs to hear others' stories as well – and the more colourful and varied the better. Real-life stories convey values, wisdom, and insights in a way that allows your boy to reflect upon them and deeply consider what sort of man he wants to become.

Challenge

All traditional Rites of Passage (ROP) required boys to perform some sort of challenge. This was the pinnacle of the ROP transition from boy to man. A boy had to do something which forced him to face his mortality, defining him as a man. This sort of challenge was often extremely dangerous with the possibility of serious injury or even death.

These days we simply cannot even consider creating challenges for boys that are dangerous. We must ensure that our boys are kept safe at all times. We must also realise that there are different levels of challenges that will be appropriate for different boys.

Try and create challenges where boys do things they would not have ordinarily thought that they could do. One of my favourite challenges is for a boy to spend time alone in nature. This will allow him to be at one with his thoughts – many boys will have never done this before! It is also the perfect time to challenge him to think about what sort of man he wants to be, what is important to him, and what he is ready to let go of from his childhood. The time alone can be anywhere from a couple of hours to a couple of days. The outdoor adventure organisation Outward Bound conducts programs that involve boys being on their own for three days. A tent or shelter is built and sufficient food and supplies are taken but the boys are otherwise alone.

There are countless other types of challenges that could be utilised. On a fishing trip the challenge may be to take responsibility and drive the boat safely on the river. In the mountains it may be to go for an all-day or overnight hike. If you are fortunate enough to travel overseas you could go bungy-jumping, or white-water river rafting, or climbing. The options are endless. What's important is not the danger or difficulty of the challenge but rather the *perception* that your boy is doing something different, something outside of his normal comfort zone.

As I have already mentioned, if we don't provide formal challenges for our boys at this age, they will likely seek dangerous risk-taking behaviours for themselves. They want to feel like men and will do reckless things which bring them face to face with their mortality.

> Gary, a businessman, describes his teenage years. 'I was drinking, driving cars really fast and trying to get them up on two wheels. I surfed on the roof of cars going over the harbour bridge and jumped out of trees ... never thinking about the consequences. On reflection I was really lucky I didn't get killed, or kill someone else.'

We have a moral responsibility to create appropriate challenges for our boys, to supervise them, and ensure there's a safety net so that they're able to accomplish something realistic without risking injury. Those running a Rite of Passage must ensure the challenge is powerful but also safe.

A teenager who succeeds at challenges will develop a sense of himself as a competent and effective individual. His Personal Identity will improve and it is unlikely he will feel the need to constantly 'prove' he is a man by engaging in unnecessary risk-taking behaviour.

Recognising and encouraging him to pursue his unique gifts and talents

When we honour and recognise a young man's unique gifts and talents in front of other men, we give him something that will help him throughout his life. Create a special space and time for this to occur. At our camps, we often decorate a chair so that it feels more like a throne and the boys sit on that in front of all the other boys and men. Don't over-plan what you are going to say: be spontaneous and just let the words flow. Don't tell him what he should or shouldn't do, or who he should or shouldn't become. Don't compare yourself to him. Just name all the positive traits you see, the gifts that he has and why you love him. It's not about what he has done but who he actually is. It doesn't really matter that he won a trophy playing soccer, what's more important is that he tries hard at soccer and is a team player. Be straight up and be honest. You don't have to make things up in order for to him to feel better about himself. You *will* find great things to talk about: I'm still to meet a young man who didn't have special gifts and talents.

It is great if you can also get other men to honour your boy for the gifts and talents they see in him. Often they will have noticed important and profound things that you may not have mentioned. Finally why not see if any of the boys want to say something. I am constantly amazed by what wonderful things boys have to say to each other when they get the chance and the environment is right.

The return

Traditional societies always celebrated the end of the Boy-to-Man Rite of Passage (ROP) with a feast, music, dancing and other fun activities. They were celebrating the successful return of the young men who were so important to their collective future. When your son returns from his Boy-to-Man ROP make sure you celebrate his accomplishment. Invite relatives, friends and people who have been pivotal or have taken an interest in his life. It is a celebration of him becoming a young man so it is a great time to honour him and reflect again on his special and unique gifts. Don't expect him to necessarily want to talk a lot about what he has just done or even how he is feeling. Give him time and don't pressure him. He'll talk when he's ready.

Change things if you can when he gets home. As I have said, significant shifts in the relationships between mother and son as well as the father and son must now occur. Parents or carers will quite rightly expect a greater level of respect and maturity from their son. It is the time to give him more privileges and extend the boundaries of what he is allowed to do. If he wants to go out on the weekends or at night this is a perfect time to allow that to happen but on the condition that you both agree what is the responsible way for him to do it. Physical changes in the environment, like changing his bedroom, can also help this process. He will need more autonomy and more privacy, and you must stop treating him like a boy, smothering him, or trying to control him. The new family dynamics must be built on mutual respect, love and healthy communication.

After his Rite of Passage, your son will not suddenly have transformed into a man who is mature, settled and has his whole future worked out. He still has to learn how to move into his new role in life. He may well slip back and display behaviours that will make you wonder whether he ever actually did his Rite of Passage and whether it had any effect! Believe me that it did and there has been a seed planted and you will see it grow and bear fruit over time.

The role of mentors post-Rite of Passage

In traditional societies, after the return, the responsibility of teaching and disciplining the young men would now fall to the older men. They would actively become involved in the young men's lives to show them the ways of the community and pass on those skills that had been handed down from generation to generation. When your son returns from his ROP, identify those men who you trust and encourage your son to spend time with them. Encourage him to seek them out for advice and support if there is something that he is struggling with or if he doesn't want to speak to you. It's a great thing to know that he has someone to talk to when he's got a problem. If you can, help him to create a network of caring, trustworthy older men that he can spend time with. It will be great for him and the older men will benefit too.

Following-up after a Rite of Passage

I cannot emphasise enough how important it is to create various forms of follow-up after a Rite of Passage. It will have been an enormous event in the life of your son and you want it to keep going in the right direction. Try to find a way to set up a regular meeting with as many people as possible who have been on the Rite of Passage. Make a space where you can sit together and have meaningful conversations. This is a chance for everyone – young and old – to discuss what's been happening. It's a chance for the young men to talk about what is going well but also where they are struggling and may need support. It's a time when they can speak to older men who they trust and respect. Importantly, it is also a time when the commitments that were made on the Rite of Passage are refreshed and new ones can also be made.

These follow-up meetings don't just have to be all about talking and serious stuff. Get creative! Go to the beach, go camping or for a hike in the mountains, go karting, meet at different people's houses … or whatever works into your family's schedule.

Creating and being involved in a Boy-to-Man ROP may be one of the most challenging things you will ever do but it will also be one of the most rewarding. All sorts of unexpected outcomes will emerge. From my experience it is by far the best thing you could ever do for your boy and the other boys in your community.

Key Points from Chapter 14

- The separation requires time away

- The transition contains the elements of storytelling, a challenge, and recognition of the boy's unique gifts and talents

- The return should be witnessed and celebrated

- Mentors and follow-up after a Rite of Passage are essential

CONCLUSION

Each of our boys and young men is unique. We all want to see them happy and successful and we all want to keep them out of trouble. If we as their parents, carers, or mentors can help them nurture their true gifts, their personal genius and spirit, and encourage them to live their lives to the fullest, then the potential for all of society to thrive is limitless.

As I have said throughout this book, after decades of working with teenage boys, I honestly believe that they are naturally loving, energetic, funny, creative and sensitive. They are passionate, they love to laugh, they can see the funny side of almost anything and they can surprise us with their wisdom. They are inspired and motivated and want to change the world. They are aware and loyal, and have a strong sense of what is right and what is wrong.

Teenage boys *are* innately good, but ensuring they stay that way is more challenging than it has ever been. They need our help, understanding and support in order to navigate the most significant transition of their lives. In the fast-paced digital age there are so many potential pitfalls, not least of all technology, drugs and mental health issues, that can threaten their personal wellbeing.

We have the power to help, we have done the research, and we understand what they are going through. Commonsense and consistent parenting based on love and respect are great places to start.

However, just as our boys change, so must we. Our roles as parents or carers, friends or relatives have to evolve when our sons become young men. We can no longer treat them like little boys – telling them what to do and how to be. We can no longer expect them to idolise us. Dads must shift the balance of power, support their sons, and ditch the old ways of relating to them. Mums need to let go of their little boys – which can be heart-wrenching – but in return welcome inspired and respectful young men who will be keen to create new, lifelong and loving relationships.

The shift from boy psychology to healthy man psychology will change your son's life forever. The more fully he can accomplish this shift, the better his future will be. Living in healthy man psychology will give him a way of being in the world that will create happiness and success – not just for him but for everyone he comes in contact with. The world needs more of these sorts of balanced and well-adjusted young men!

With our support and encouragement, our sons' well-being on the PI scale will improve. They will develop and enjoy healthy family relationships, acquire valuable life skills, and reap the benefits of good physical health. They will recognise and appreciate their unique gifts and talents – and so will everyone else.

Finally, a Rite of Passage properly conducted contains all the elements necessary for your boy to make the healthy transition to a young man. He will be supported from then on not only by you but by a network of mentors and other members of the community who genuinely care about his wellbeing.

I hope this book has moved you and inspired you to act. Our future and that of our boys' depends on it.

ACKNOWLEDGEMENTS

Many people have been involved directly or indirectly in the writing of this book.

To those who physically helped me by reading, brainstorming and editing. Nicky Reavley, Josephine Dee Barrett, Susannah Rubinstein, Rod Morrison and Lucy. Thank you for your wisdom, patience and faith. I must have been a nightmare to work with at times but we also had lots of fun and I am happy to be able to call all of you friends.

To Rein Van de Ruit who has mentored me for twenty years and continues to support and inspire me to stay on my path. You have given me so much knowledge in the form of countless books, magazines and CDs on the subject of Rites of Passage and the development of the human psyche. Your generosity of spirit is incredible and I can truly say that none of this work would have happened if you had not been there to encourage me at the beginning.

To the incredible men and women I have worked with in the last twenty years creating and running youth programs all over Australia and internationally. I honour all of you especially those who continue to do this work despite the challenges involved and the lack of financial support. I know that many of you have made great sacrifices in order to do what you believe is so important. We have had some incredible adventures, created all sorts of mayhem, and changed the lives of thousands of people. There are too many of you to name but I know that as a result of your continuing dedication, Rites of Passage are slowly but surely becoming a mainstream event. Also to all those who just got in there and in their own way helped it all to happen. Bere, James Dodds, Elvian Drysdale, Maree Lipschitz, John Imbrogno, Simone Verdon, Joseph Raya, Annelise Kaufman, Mark Emerson, Stephen Moss, Stephane Chatonsky, Garry Thomson, Karim, Kristin Canning, Jess Gilmore, Suzie Tieman, Caroline Pegram, Ranald Allan, Marybeth Zang and a whole heap of other people.

To all those who financially supported the work and put their organisational resources and time behind helping us to scale. Michael Traill, Jan Owen, Daniel Petre, Robert Bleakley, George Lewin, Richard Howes, Chris Cuffe, David Vaux, James Hodgkinson, Michael Price, Julie White, Gianni Zappala, James Tait, Caroline Stewart and many more.

To the young men who have been on our programs. Your courage, honesty, wisdom and passion for life is what drives all we do. I have been so privileged to meet you and bear witness to the amazing transformations you go through. Every time I go on a camp I leave more deeply inspired to continue this work. I also love that many of you keep in contact and that we have become friends.

To my father, who has been an unwavering source of encouragement to bloody well get this book done. You have always wanted the best for me and have an unlimited stream of thoughts and ideas as to what I can do. I know how happy you will be the day this book is finally published.

To my mother, who has loved me unconditionally since the day I was born. My respect and love for you is 'to the moon and back'. You are the best.

Finally, to my sons Jarrah and Jaden. I am so proud to have you both in my life. You are the most amazing sons a father could ever wish for. I appreciate our relationship, I enjoy the adventures we continue to have together and I love each of you more than anything in the world … though I do struggle a bit with the fact that you are now bigger, faster and stronger than me; it seems a little bit unfair!

PARENTING SUPPORT RESOURCES

LINKS

Links were correct at the time of printing; please check my website for updates www.doctorarne.com

Advice on Parenting
www.parentfurther.com

Australian Indigenous Health Info Net
www.healthinfonet.ecu.edu.au

Building Healthy Family Relationships
www.aifs.gov.au/institute/pubs/factssheets/familytime.html

Consciously Parenting Australia
www.consciouslyparenting.com.au

Combatting depression – and achieving a healthy Personal Identity
www.gallup.com/poll/14986/how-many-teens-mood-medication.aspx
www.stats.org/stories/2004/antidepressants_suicide_oct05_04.htm
www.ei-resource.org/articles/mental-and-emotional-problem-articles/
easy-and-natural-ways-to-raise-low-serotonin-levels
healthyliving.azcentral.com/natural-ways-increase-serotonin-
endorphins-8991.html

Family Parenting Courses – Relationships Australia
www.relationships.org.au

Father/Son Relationship

www.aifs.gov.au/institute/pubs/factssheets/familytime.html

Fathers To Be

www.fatherstobe.org

Gen Z and the Digital Age

en.wikipedia.org/wiki/Generation_Z

ncsu.edu/iei/index.php/emerging-issues/generation-z

www.jwtintelligence.com/tag/gen-z/

www.hrpulse.co.za/toolbox/228841-7-generation-z-facts

www.sharpermindcenters.com/side_affects.htm

www.dailymail.co.uk/news/article-2198450

pewinternet.org/Reports/2012/Teens-and-smartphones/Cell-phone-ownership.aspx?view=all

news.cnet.com/8301-1035_3-57510060-94/

teens-grab-up-smartphones-faster-than-other-age-groups

www.sciencedaily.com/releases/2012/10/121009112138.htm

The Kids Are All Right – Parenting Teenagers in Australia

www.thekidsareallright.com.au

Mankind Project

www.mkpau.org

Old Me, New Me

www.oldmenewme.com

Outward Bound

www.outwardbound.org.au

Parenting and Child Health – Services – Parenting Groups

www.cyh.com

Parenting Support Groups

www.ask.com

Finding parenting courses / Find parenting programs / Help for parents

www.parentline.org.au

The Pathways Foundation

www.pathwaysfoundation.com.au

The Positive Parenting Network of Australia

www.parent.net.au

Powerhouse Programs

www.powerhouseprograms.com.au

Raising Children Network

www.raisingchildren.net.au

The Real Impact of the Digital Age on our Young Men

elkhorn.unl.edu/epublic/pages/publicationD.jsp?publicationId=790ß
www.edinformatics.com

Self-Empowerment for Children

www.charansurdhar.com

Steve Biddulph's website and articles

www.stevebiddulph.com

Support Groups – Attachment Parenting Australia

www.attachmentparentingaustralia.com

Uplifting Australia

www.upliftingaustralia.com.au

Australian Rite of Passage Programs

www.doctorarne.com
www.upliftingaustralia.com.au
www.pathwaysfoundation.com.au
www.theritejourney.com.au
www.powerhouseprograms.com.au

International Rite of Passage Programs

New Zealand

www.tracks.net.nz

www.tides.net.nz

USA

www.schooloflostborders.org

www.goldenbridge.org

www.riteofpassagejourneys.org

www.ritesofpassagenw.com

www.malespirituality.org

www.ritesofpassagevisionquest.org

www.riteofpassage.com

www.earthpeoplesunited.org

www.db55.org

www.ritesofpassageonline.org

United Kingdom

www.journeymanuk.org

www.ritesofpassage.uk.com

www.wholeland.org.uk

www.chanceforchange.org.uk

www.wildgenie.com

www.wildnature.org.uk

www.campbeaumont.co.uk

www.newinitiatives.co.uk

Europe

www.campbeaumont.fr

FURTHER READING

There are many great books about parenting boys/young men and Rites of Passage. I suggest you read as many as possible and trust your judgement as to which make the most sense for you and your situation. Here are a few that have been particularly helpful to me during my career and the writing of this book.

Biddulph, S. (2004) *Manhood – Why Boys Are Different – And How to Help Them Become Happy And Well-Balanced Men*, Vermilion Press, London, UK.

Biddulph, S. (2008) *Raising Boys – An Action Plan For Changing Men's Lives*, Celestial Arts, Berkley, USA.

Bly, R. (1990) *Iron John – A Book About Men*, Addison-Wesley Publishing, New York, USA.

Carr-Greg, M. & Shale, E. (2002) *Adolescence – A Guide for Parents*, Finch Publishing, Sydney, Australia.

Cohen, D. (1991) *The Circle of Life – Rituals from the Human Family Album*, Harper San Francisco, USA.

Gennep, A.V. (1960) *The Rites of Passage*, Routledge Library Editions, Abingdon, UK.

Gliksman, M. (2003) *Bad Boy*, Penguin Books, Melbourne, Australia.

Goleman, D. (2006) *Emotional Intelligence*, Bantam Dell Publishing, New York, USA.

Lashlie, C. (2005) *He'll Be OK – Growing Gorgeous Boys Into Good Men*, HarperCollins Publishers, Auckland, NZ.

Levant, R.F. & Pollack, W.S. (2003) *A New Psychology of Men*, Basic Books, New York, USA.

Mahdi, L.C. (1994) *Betwixt & Between: Patterns of Masculine and Feminine Initiation*, Open Court Publishing Company, Chicago, USA.

Moore, R. & Gillette, D. (1991) *King, Warrior, Magician, Lover: Rediscovering the Archetypes of the Mature Masculine*, HarperCollins Publishers, New York, USA.

Moore, R.L. (2001) *The Archetype of Initiation: Sacred Space, Ritual Process, and Personal Transformation. Lectures and Essays*, Xlibris Corporation, USA.

Pink, D.H. (2006) *A Whole New Mind*, The Berkley Publishing Group, New York, USA.

Pollack, W.S. & Shuster, T. (2000) *Real Boys' Voices*, Random House, New York, USA.

Real, T. (1998) *I Don't Want to Talk About It*, Scribner, New York, USA.

Robinson, J.C. Ph.D. (1995) *Death of a Hero, Birth of the Soul*, Council Oak, Oakland, USA.

Rohr, R. (1992) *The Wild Man's Journey – Reflections on Male Spirituality*, St. Anthony Messenger Press, Cincinnati, USA.

Stephenson, B. (2006) *From Boys to Men*, Park Street Press, Rochester, USA.

Weiner, B. (1992) *Boy into Man – A Father's Guide to Initiation of Teenage Sons*, Transformation Press, Berkeley, USA.

Ykeema, F. (2013) *Rock & Water, Skills for Physical-Social Teaching with Boys*, Gadaku Institute, BN Schagen, the Netherlands.

INDEX

ADHD, 55

alcohol, xv, xvii, 51, 55, 84, 86, 96–102, 112, 165, 194

anti-depressants *see also* drugs, 55, 105

balance of power, 116, 125–128, 247

Biddulph, Steve, xiii–xvi, 112

boy psychology *see also* healthy man psychology, 16–37, 208–209, 221, 248

brain development, 45, 77, 100, 180–181

bullying *see also* cyber bullying, 76, 130

collaboration, 164, 176–177, 218–219

communication, xviii, 5, 10, 39, 51, 75, 80, 89–92, 94, 96, 217, 244

mother/son, 157–158

cyber bullying *see also* bullying, 57, 59, 62

depression, 1, 33, 36, 55, 86, 103–106, 122, 129, 180

digital age, 54–63, 86, 180, 247

'digital divide', 60

drugs, xiii, xviii, 24, 40, 41, 47, 55, 73, 83–84, 86, 87, 97, 99–102, 111, 112, 155, 194, 247

emotional changes, 44

EQ (Emotional Intelligence), 166, 171–174, 217–219

exercise, 181

experimentation, 40, 73, 100–101

extended adolescence, 36

families, 9–12, 22, 60, 96, 205, 224

father/son relationship *see also* mother/son relationship, 140–162

gaming, 48, 60–61, 112, 189

Generation Z, 54–57

gifts and talents
recognising your son's, 120–125
Rite of Passage, 242
girls, 10, 13, 39, 43–44, 45, 47, 58
GQ (Generational Intelligence),
166, 172–175, 218–219

happiness and success, 2, 5–8, 10,
14, 30–34, 86, 173, 248
healthy food, 178, 218
healthy man psychology *see also* boy
psychology, 16–37, 208–209,
221, 248
healthy Personal Identity *see also*
Personal Identity (PI) scale, 80,
86, 88, 101, 102, 170, 177, 179,
213, 218, 241

indigenous societies *see* traditional
societies
internet, 54–63, 97, 229
IQ (Intelligence Quotient),
171–174

Kaufman, Gershen, 130

life skills, 77, 85, 88, 90, 94, 95,
137, 163–177, 217, 248
'lift-off', 3–5
living in the moment, 5–8
Louv, Richard, 181

men behaving like boys, 30–34
mentors, 52, 92, 192, 134–140,
213, 219, 222, 225, 244
mother/son relationship *see
also* father/son relationship,
110–139

nature (outdoors), 29, 178,
181–183, 217, 240

parenting
teenagers, 74–81, 113–115
young boys, 73, 114,
143–145
Personal Identity (PI) scale *see
also* healthy Personal Identity,
87–96, 101, 153, 163, 215, 248
physical changes, 41–43
physical health, 178
Rite of Passage, 218–219
Pollack, William, 111
pornography, 43, 58, 62
pressure
marketing, 107–108
mental, 46–47
modern day, 11
peer group, 55, 97, 101,
103, 107–109
privileges and responsibilities, 48,
77, 127, 165–168, 217–218, 243
puberty, 3, 10, 16, 32, 36, 41, 44,
45, 50, 97, 125

relationships
    family, 216–217
    quality, 6, 8
    women, 17, 29–30, 151–155
resilience, 53, 166, 169–171,
    217–218
Rites of Passage (ROP), 2, 3, 4, 8,
    9, 36, 51–53, 185, 201–226
    follow-up, 245
    impact, 215–220
    implementing, 227–247
    'return', 210
    'separation', 209, 234–235
    story, 189–200
    timing, 229–230
    'transition', 209, 238–243
rituals, 36, 202, 204, 206, 209, 211
ROP *see* Rites of Passage

sex, 13, 42, 44, 57, 145, 203
'sexting', 57
shaming, 27, 78, 128–131, 169
single fathers, 12, 131–133, 231
single mothers, 12, 157–161, 214,
    231
sleep, 1, 12, 56–57, 178, 180, 217
social networking, 60–61, 91, 180, 181
spiritual changes, 41, 45
SQ (Social Intelligence), 164,
    171–174, 217–218
suicide, 2, 57, 104

'techno creators', 61–62
'techno slaves', 60–62
television, 20, 27, 32, 72, 74, 92,
    97, 99, 107, 130, 132, 142, 150,
    166, 180
temper tantrums, 17, 27, 28,
    38–40, 46, 145, 151, 152, 154,
    164, 172, 228
text messaging *see also* 'sexting', 56,
    57, 60, 180
Tolle, Eckhart, 7
traditional societies, 3, 36, 49,
    37, 136, 203–204, 207–208,
    210–211, 219, 226, 229, 235,
    239, 243, 244

van Gennep, Arnold, 205, 209

why boys muck up, 38–41
world of men, bringing your son
    into, 116–120